LEAD

WITH

EMPATHY

ELEVATE YOUR LEADERSHIP & MANAGEMENT SKILLS, BUILD STRONG TEAMS, AND INSPIRE LASTING CHANGE IN YOUR BUSINESS

PETE SRODOSKI

TABLE OF CONTENTS

INTRODUCTION

A leader is one who knows the way, goes the way, and shows the way.
–John C. Maxwell

Hello, fellow leaders! Let me welcome you to a journey that is not only going to change how you lead but also make you understand what it actually means to be an impactful leader. Try to imagine this—a leader who not only sits behind their desk, making orders like a drill sergeant. Now in place of this, try to think of a leader who cares, understands, and connects with the team in a genuine way. A leader who can easily sense the words that are left unspoken, stand in the shoes of the team, and read between the lines—that is the kind of leader we are talking about here.

You might think, *But, Pete, why should we listen to what you are saying or telling us to do?* Well, my friends, writing this book emerged from a transformative journey that spanned my personal and professional life. My aim is to make you understand the power of empathy in leadership and the way it can help revolutionize the business sector, drive lasting change, and develop strong teams. It is true that my experiences are varied, but a common thread ties them all—a realization that empathy is the ultimate key to effective leadership. Here's a quick fact for you—86% of employees have the belief that empathetic leadership can boost their morale (Ernst & Young, 2023).

With a great deal of experience as a CEO and COO in small businesses, I have cultivated the ability to inspire and guide teams in the direction of success. During my early career days, I came across a world where tattoos depicted unprofessionalism. In fact, even in today's world, 76% of employees feel their tattoos might impact their careers (AIMS Education, 2015). It is mostly aligned with societal expectations. The struggle to keep a balance between my true self and societal expectations resulted in curiosity regarding changing the dynamics of workplace culture.

Do you know what the turning point was? It was when the policy shift of PetSmart permitted me to embrace all my tattoos openly. It is what pushed me to question the role of empathy in reshaping the norms. Empathy also helped me get out of the grip of panic attacks and anxiety. Dealing with all such challenges made me understand the profound role of empathy, both outward and self-directed, in developing a workplace culture that is supportive and safe. My extensive journey from avoidance to resilience taught me how empathy can be used to break down barriers and foster courage and growth.

You can say that this book is a way of recounting all my career stories that involve resilience, transformation, and growth with the aim of inspiring managers and leaders to embrace the impact of empathy in the workplace. The aim of this book is to kindle a sense of empathy in the reader's mind, resulting in a necessary shift in their approach to leading a team.

For me, empathy is a lot more than just a skill. It is a strategic imperative. The experiences I had made me understand that true leadership transcends conventional norms to embrace empathy as a force of transformation. Such a realization helped in fueling my determination to change my style of leadership, resulting in professional and personal growth.

Now right before you make up your mind to picture a group hug session in the meeting room (we are not there yet, just kidding), let us get things straight—empathy is not at all about turning the workplace into a cozy and comfortable den of therapy. It is all about being able to find the sweet spot that lies between understanding the struggles of the team and directing them toward greatness.

Empathy can be regarded as a secret weapon of leadership. It is the weapon that would help you decode the mysterious expressions during important meetings and understand why the guy from accounting requires an extra shot of espresso on Mondays. If you have ever found yourself saying, *Why can't all of us get along?* during a team meeting, this book might turn out to be your new BFF. Hey, do not get fooled, as this book is not like an average self-help manual that will make you chant affirmations every day as you get up from bed. We will talk about real-world empathy that you will be using in your style of leadership. You will learn, and you might even get really inspired by reading some of the anecdotes that I have got for you.

Now you might think, *Can empathy truly help in being the true king of the corporate jungle?* Well, here is a secret for you. Empathy acts like the secret chocolate that you try to hide from others right at the back of the desk drawer. It might not be able to solve problems of all kinds, but it can surely make things a lot better.

The chapters of this book will take care of hard questions such as, *How am I going to handle the emotional meltdown of a team member without any need to hand out tissues like confetti?* and *How can I provide constructive feedback without triggering an existential crisis?* Get ready, my friend, as we are all set to navigate the waters of workplace drama, team-building exercises that all of us dread, and team dynamics. It does not matter whether you are a new boss, a seasoned manager, or a person who simply loves to imagine their goldfish as the best audience; get set to find out the magic that can happen when you learn to lead a team with empathy.

Make yourself comfortable, get some snacks, and let us get started with this empathy-filled adventure as a team. I am about to add a sprinkle of understanding, a dash of kindness, and a little bit of humor to your great leadership journey. So let's get started!

CHAPTER 1:
EMPATHY—THE HEARTBEAT OF EFFECTIVE LEADERSHIP

Empathy is patiently and sincerely seeing the world through the other person's eyes. It is not learned in school; it is cultivated over a lifetime.
—Albert Einstein

Hello, aspiring leaders and curious minds! Let me welcome all of you to a section where we will dive headfirst into the realm of empathy. You might think, *Why does empathy get a VIP section in a leadership guidebook?* Well, my fellow leaders, grab your bucket of popcorn as we will soon unravel why empathy acts like the secret sauce that can turn any ordinary leader into an extraordinary one.

Try to think of this—you lead a team that is similar to a buffet menu (different skill sets, quirks, and personalities). Now think of yourself trying to navigate this diverse team without a proper compass. That is what leadership without empathy would look like. It would feel like trying to set up IKEA furniture without the instruction manual.

The aim of this section is to unravel the mysteries of empathy. Empathy is like a superpower that lets you understand what is unsaid, read between the lines, and be able to connect with the team on a psychological level. No worries, as we will not be sharing stories of leadership where leaders turned into therapists (we will leave that for the movies). It is now time to make empathy the main energy of your leadership journey.

DECODING EMPATHY: MORE THAN JUST FEELING

Often we come across the saying that empathy is required in this world. There is no doubt that all of us have seen this in one form or the other a manager who is not able to link to the true struggles of a team or partners who can no longer understand one another. However, if we long for other people to take into consideration our feelings and perspectives, why do we fail to do the same?

To start with, it requires effort and time to understand why and how other people feel the way they do. To be very honest, none of us are willing to use all such resources for too many people. In fact, even when people get motivated to showcase empathy, trying to do the same is not that easy. The thing is that when we try to show empathy, the other person can feel understood. Due to this, they are more likely to reciprocate our efforts and decide to try harder from their end as well. Do you know what the end result is? Well, it would give rise to a relationship where both parties get motivated enough to provide others the benefit of the doubt and let go of small failures.

Now you might ask, *But what exactly is empathy? How can I develop it?* No worries, as I will break things for you.

What Is Empathy?

In today's society, you are most likely to get varied definitions of empathy based on the individual you ask. However, most people would agree to a little bit of variation of this—it is the "ability." In order to display and feel empathy, there is no requirement to share the same circumstances as others. It is more like an attempt to understand others in a better way simply by getting an idea of their perspective to understand and share the feelings of another (LaRusso, 2021).

Empathy comes in three parts, and each part has a formal name. However, it would be easier to understand them as *feelings*, *thoughts*, and *actions*. Whenever people try to discuss empathy, the primary focus is given to the cognitive perspective. For most of us, empathy is about putting ourselves in the shoes of others. But in order to practice empathy in the right way, all three parts are necessary (Miller, 2022):

- *Cognitive*: Cognitive empathy is the ability to understand the perspective of someone else and their feelings and thoughts. You can regard this as the thinking aspect of empathy. As the name goes by, it takes place on a cognitive level. Those who practice cognitive empathy will make educated guesses depending on the kind of past experiences and knowledge they have. You will be putting yourself in the shoes of others, as we believe empathy to be. It is one of the most important steps in practicing empathy.

- *Emotive*: Emotive empathy involves being able to feel with someone. It is a lot more than the cognitive part. The aim here is to stand as equals with others and feel with them. You might not believe this, but all of us are wired for this biologically. We have mirror neurons that get activated when we tend to experience any kind of emotion, and in the same way, they activate when we see someone else experiencing emotions. For instance, when you see someone feeling sad, the mirror neurons will activate and will let you experience sadness on the same level and be empathetic.

- *Empathic action*: You can think of this as the "doing" part. It involves a lot more than just understanding other people and being able to share what they feel. It moves us to take necessary action and help others regardless of our capabilities.

If you look at empathy from the perspective of a leader, being empathetic is all about being able to understand the emotions of the team members, challenges, and motivations and using all of these collectively to direct the actions you take. Do you know that team managers who tend to show more empathy toward the members of the team are regarded as better performers by their superiors (Leading Effectively Staff, 2023)?

SYMPATHY VERSUS EMPATHY: KNOW THE DIFFERENCE

Both sympathy and empathy are two traits that can help anyone relate to other people and also understand the perspectives of others in the workplace. Most of us tend to use these terms interchangeably, but they are a lot different from each other. Sympathy involves feeling supportive and caring for the situation of another person, whereas empathy is the power to identify and share the emotions of others. Do you get the difference?

Let me make things easier for you. For instance, sympathy can make you feel sorry for a team member when they go through a tough time. When it comes to empathy, it will help you understand their hardships and emotions as you will be thinking of yourself in the same situation. Suppose a team member of yours, let's call her Kathy, is finding it tough to find a balance between her work and caring for her sick husband. If you feel sympathetic, it will make you feel sorry for her. But when you try to be empathetic, you will get to understand her anxiety and stress as you will think of yourself in her shoes. It is said that empathy tends to encourage helping behavior a lot more than sympathy does (Greater Good in Education, n.d.).

Why Is Sympathy Not Enough?

It is true that sympathetic leaders can provide a kind response to a team member who is experiencing a hard time in life. However, if they cannot be empathetic toward the person, they cannot experience a connection with the situation. A response cannot make anything better. It is a connection that does. When you try to be an empathetic leader, you can showcase your willingness to connect with the team member you are dealing with. In place of just expressing your support, you will be able to provide real support.

Sympathetic Versus Empathetic Leadership

Suppose an employee has a sick mother at home. The employee comes to you and mentions that they haven't slept well for a couple of days as their mother needed their care all the time.

A *sympathetic* leader would respond by saying, "Having a sick mother is really tough. I am really sorry to hear this. But the good news is that there is no important presentation for your clients this month. I have got a presentation to finish and that is why I also cannot sleep properly for the last few days. At least you don't have to prepare a presentation." While the leader showed some concern and could relate to the exhaustion of the team member; they ended up minimizing the experience of the employee. They did so by making their situation look worse. It is said that an empathetic leader would never use the term "at least" as this might dismiss the difficulty that the other person is experiencing.

But if the leader was *empathetic*, they would have responded by saying, "I am well aware of how tough it might be to handle work when you are running on little rest. I have experienced this kind of exhaustion many times. Do you think I can support you in any way with all your ongoing projects so that you don't feel burnt out?" An empathetic leader would try their best to show that they understand the position of the employee and would also reach out to support them.

Empathy as an Expression of Understanding

Empathy entails deep understanding without passing any kind of judgment. There is no need to completely agree with the worldview, behavior, or religion of the other person in order to express empathy. Empathy tends to happen when you, as a leader, can sense and respond to the experiences of the other person simply by the creation of space for that individual so that they can feel valued, heard, and understood. You will get to communicate your emotional understanding as you try to be fully present in this way.

Keep in mind that you will need to resist the urge to solve issues of the other person or offer any kind of solution. The more someone tries to help, the less empathetic they will be. If you fail to do so, you will be doing nothing other than shifting to sympathy. Having the willingness to understand and learn is all about listening to the perspective of others and understanding their whys. You can think of empathy as committed listening that comes without any kind of agenda. The only thing that empathy might cost you is the energy of being present fully.

EMPATHY AND EMOTIONAL INTELLIGENCE: TWO SIDES OF THE SAME COIN

Emotional intelligence (EQ) can be regarded as the navigation system for your emotions. EQ helps in understanding your feelings, managing them, and also reading the emotional signs of other people. But are you aware of the relationship between EQ and empathy? EQ and empathy are like jelly and peanut butter. They go hand in hand like Robin and Batman (you can keep the capes aside, of course). We already know that empathy is what helps us understand what other people are feeling, and EQ helps in the management of your own emotions and responding in the right way.

Try to think of this—you are at work and a member of your team is experiencing an emotional meltdown because of a failed presentation. Your radar of empathy gets activated and you start sensing their distress. But you should also thank your EQ as you don't freak out or join hands with your team member for the meltdown party. In place of doing so, you offer them a listening ear along with a proper plan that would help them handle the situation. See, you just showed how these two superheroes work in partnership. Empathy and EQ are meant for everyday superheroes like you and me.

Key Elements of Emotional Intelligence

Are you aware of the key elements of EQ? If not, let me share them with you.

- *Self-awareness*: This is the ability to identify and understand your emotions. It is one of the most critical skills of EQ. Besides helping in recognizing your emotions, self-awareness can also help in making you aware of your moods, actions, and emotions on other people. In order to be self-aware, you will have to be capable enough to monitor your own emotions.

- *Self-regulation*: EQ needs you to regulate and manage your emotions. Self-regulation does not indicate that you will have to put all your emotions on lockdown and hide what you truly feel. All it indicates is waiting for the perfect time and place to express them.

- *Social skills*: Genuine emotional understanding would involve a lot more than simple understanding of your emotions and that of others. You will also have to put this into work on a daily basis. So being able to interact with other people is a necessary skill of EQ. Skills like verbal and nonverbal communication, active listening, and persuasiveness would let you develop meaningful connections with others.

- *Empathy*: Being empathetic would let you understand the power dynamics that could easily influence social connections. It is necessary to guide your daily interactions with different people.

Did you know that 90% of top performers in the workplace come with high EQ (Bradberry, n.d.)? This demonstrates the importance of EQ and also empathy in leadership.

THE POWER OF EMPATHY IN LEADERSHIP

Alright, my fellow leaders, let us talk about a leadership power that will not need any flying or capes. Yes, I am talking about empathy. You might think, *Isn't empathy meant for therapists?* Well, empathy is a lot more than listening and nodding. Empathy in leadership is more or less like having a secret decoder ring for the thoughts and feelings of your team. You need to trust me here, as once you wield this power, it will act like magic that would turn, "Oh no, it is Monday again," to, "Let's go, team!"

Let us be real here, all of us have experienced an ice-cold manager who tends to give out orders as if they are reading a grocery list. Reflecting on my journey, I realized that a lack of empathy in my style of leadership acted like a major roadblock to developing true connections and enhancing growth.

During the early days of my career, the majority of my approach was influenced by societal expectations and norms. All I wanted to be was the epitome of professionalism, having the belief that authenticity and vulnerability should not be allowed in the workplace. Such a disconnect between my leadership style and true self ended up developing a huge barrier.

Going back to the ice-cold manager, I have experienced it myself. If you ask such a person for any sort of guidance, they would answer with jargon, or if you try to share a concern, they would reply with a memo. You can never call it leadership, my friend. That is nothing more than a form of automated response system.

Now picture a leader who not only listens to you but truly hears what you say. Sounds like a dream, right? This may be someone who understands the frustration when the internet crashes during an important meeting or someone who understands that, at times, a bad mood is a lot more than a bad mood—it could be the result of a flat tire, a cup of spilled coffee, or a burnt toast. You will have to understand that empathy can act as the backstage ticket to the true and human side of leadership style. It is more or less having an easy cheat code for the development of genuine connections that extend far beyond project timelines. You will not be the boss; you will be a person who will actually understand why David from marketing might require a day off after the bad presentation.

Empathy Is Not a Quick Fix

Let us not kid ourselves, as empathy cannot be regarded as a quick fix for all sorts of workplace mishaps. It is not something that would balance the spreadsheets on its own or would extend the deadlines magically. However, what it can do is develop a team that is filled with motivation, a team that is collaborative, and a team with a higher chance of remembering your birthday. How can someone tap into this empathy thing? All it involves is active listening, putting oneself in the shoes of others, and understanding that every member of the team has got a story. It is about embracing the idea that emotions do not act like the enemy; it acts as the glue that can hold a team together.

Traits of an Empathetic Leader

Let's have a look at some of the most common traits of an empathetic leader:

- *Active listening*: In place of simply listening to all that is being said, an empathetic leader would try to process the meanings of every word and also the requirements behind them. Such a leader would try their best to be engaged and fully present in the conversation. Responding to something is not their goal; trying to understand is.

- *Awareness of perspective*: An empathetic leader would always try to look at situations from various angles or perspectives. The best thing about an empathetic leader is that they would consider every circumstance in an objective way, trying to go deep into the matter to develop a genuine image.

- *Authenticity*: The way in which someone expresses externally should also align with internal values. An empathetic leader will always be true to themselves in the way they react to other people. They would not say anything that would exacerbate a situation.

EMPATHY: A SKILL THAT CAN BE DEVELOPED

Most people think of empathy as a special skill that some people possess by birth. No, that's not the case. It is not only reserved for those who come with a halo over their heads. You will have to understand that it is a skill that can be learned just like any other skill. You can learn and polish it until you turn yourself into an empathy black belt holder (just kidding).

Before you start to think of yourself sitting on the top of a mountain, chanting mantras of empathy under the light of the moon, let us pause for a moment. Most of us regard developing empathy as being a Zen master overnight. But it is more like learning how to ride a bicycle. The only difference is that in place of pedals, you will use understanding, and in place of balance, you will try not to crash into the awkwardness of emotional gossip.

Picture this—you are right in the middle of a full-fledged workplace debate, with opinions flying here and there at a faster rate than a game of dodgeball. Your team member, Steven, seems like he is ready to explode from frustration. Now if you are an empathetic leader, you would not only focus on the agitation of Steven, but you will also try to understand where it is coming from. You might even try to defuse the debate by using a well-timed joke about snacks in the office (no one can resist the power of a great snack).

So how can someone get into the realm of empathy? It is similar to going to an emotional gym, where you will start with small weights and slowly work your way up to heavier weights. You can start by listening actively when a member of your team talks. I am talking about eye contact, nodding, and keeping your phone away from being a distracting element. Next, put on your detective hat and try to have a look at the body language. Are they sweating? Are they clenching their fists?

How can you forget the "I get it" language? Suppose your team member says, "My alarm didn't ring this morning, and I was also stuck in a traffic jam." You might reply by saying, "Yeah, I know. That happens." Well, it is more or less like handing over a cup of empathy tea. In place of saying so, try, "I know. That's the worst. I can also recall the time when my alarm failed to ring, and I ended up singing in the car. Do you know who the audience was? Well, it was traffic." Kaboom! Now they are sipping a hot cup of "you got me" latte.

The next time you go through the complicated maze of human emotions, keep in mind that empathy is a lot more than a mystical power that is only meant for a few. It is a life skill, a leadership element.

Happy empathizing, my leaders!

CHAPTER 2:
MIRROR, MIRROR—THE EMPATHETIC LEADER'S SELF-REFLECTION

Whenever you are about to find fault with someone, ask yourself the following question: What fault of mine most nearly resembles the one I am about to criticize? —Marcus Aurelius

Before you start to imagine whether we would talk about Snow White's tale, let me tell you that we will not talk about magical mirrors that would keep providing compliments (I know that would be a great workplace accessory). We will discuss a completely different form of reflection—the good old self-reflection, with a touch of empathy. You can think of this as a personal session of therapy without the soothing background music and a cozy couch.

You must have heard of the saying that in order to understand other people, you will have to understand yourself in the first place. No worries, as I am here to break things up for you without any kind of philosophical melodrama. You can think of this as a journey where you and your mirror will turn into BFFs.

You must have understood by now that empathetic leadership is not about reading a room like a detective. It always starts with getting to know your own self—your quirks, your strengths, and also your flaws. It is about acknowledging the fact that you also are a human being who is prone to make occasional mistakes and the urge to binge-watch videos on super stressful days.

So grab your mirror, dust off your self-awareness, and let us get started with this self-reflection journey.

THE POWER OF SELF-REFLECTION IN LEADERSHIP

Do you know what leads the way to honest leadership? Yes, you guessed it right—self-reflection. With the help of daily self-reflection, a leader can strengthen their self-awareness. You might think, *But what is the need for self-reflection?* Well, the answer is quite simple. It is a tool that tends to infuse humility into an individual and help them get to know their weaknesses, strengths, and also areas that can be improved.

There is no doubt that leadership is a tough game where you, as a leader, will have to take care of multiple roles like budgeting, management, paperwork, hiring, resolving conflicts, motivating the team, and a lot more. Trying to balance responsibilities of these kinds can turn out to be pretty stressful and would need a combination of special qualities such as passion, confidence, patience, transparency, and integrity.

A leader comes with various qualities, among which self-reflection is indispensable for me. It is something that can make a true leader stand out of the crowd. A leader who does not focus on self-reflection will end up affecting their internal growth along with the growth of the team.

What Is Self-Reflection?

It is the method of observing oneself to get to know the weaknesses and strengths and develop into a better person (Habash, 2022). Simply by getting a proper understanding of oneself, an individual can determine the steps that would be the right options to attain professional and personal growth. The self-reflection process would involve introspection into the kind of person you are, the person you would like to change into, and the steps that you will take to attain the goals.

Keep in mind that the time you invest in self-reflection should never be regarded as unproductive. It is a valuable exercise where you will think about the qualities you possess and start acting on all your weaknesses.

What Can Be Gained From Self-Reflection?

The benefits for leaders are innumerable when it comes to self-reflection. Let's have a look at some of the most common benefits of self-reflection:

- *Emotional intelligence*: When you practice self-reflection on a daily basis, it can help in boosting your emotional intelligence. When internal qualities are examined, it can help in the development of two components of EQ in your personality. They are self-awareness and self-regulation. Simply by the development of self-awareness, anyone can get to understand their weaknesses and strengths in a better way. It will provide you a better understanding of your emotions and what drives your goals and beliefs.

    Did you know that self-awareness can help in understanding the impact of all the actions that you take on other people? Yes, you heard me right. With the help of self-regulation, you can control your emotions that are disruptive in nature and also adapt to all sorts of circumstances. With the help of these emotional components, you can take your leadership skills to a whole new level.

- *Confidence*: A true leader needs to have strong self-confidence to lead an organization in the direction of success. Confidence is something that can help in the improvement of communication along with decision-making. You will get to discard all your negative traits and see yourself emerge as a better and more confident leader with the help of self-reflection.

- *Integrity*: You will get to look deep into the values you hold. Self-reflection would let you throw light on all those areas of your personality that require improvement. It would help you in getting a better understanding of your morals and values. In fact, you can get a better picture of how you need to change yourself. There will be times when you will have to deal with stressful events or situations as a leader. When you hold a clear understanding of your core values, you will strengthen your integrity. Making better decisions will become a piece of cake. You will get to review all the decisions that you took in the past and improve your process of making decisions for the future.

When you start practicing self-reflection, you will turn into a different kind of leader—a leader who does not blame external factors for the failure of a project. For instance, you will get to reflect on the process of your team and get to know areas of improvement instead of trying to blame external factors for a failed project.

Using Self-Reflection for Improving Leadership

Do you desire to be a team leader who can inspire other people? You will have to use self-reflection. You will get to make better decisions as self-reflection will provide you with an open mind, and your team members will trust you more as they will see you are always open to listening to them.

Here are some of the ways in which you can practice self-reflection at the workplace:

- Always make important decisions while keeping others in mind, such as how the decision might affect their work–life balance.
- Take the necessary time to understand the viewpoints and needs of your team members.
- Let yourself and your team members express what they feel without any sort of judgment.
- Always be honest with both your team members and yourself when you feel upset or stressed.
- Never hesitate to express your ideas or to be true to oneself.
- Never forget to bring the values you hold to work.

The above mentioned tips might seem a bit daunting as you look at them for the first time. But you can always take the help of others who can provide you with guidance for the creation of strategies to improve self-awareness.

Whenever someone from my team encounters a failure, I ask myself, *Where exactly did I fail them?* I lead my team with the belief that a good leader should always look internally first when anything goes wrong. Most people I have worked for in my career failed to see how their own actions have resulted in team failures. It is necessary to reflect on any failure in the first place before you get to coach your team. Lose all the ego you have and look out for new opportunities.

I once worked for a company whose CEO was a narcissist by nature. That person had an inflated sense of ego and took credit when the team performed well. There was a moment when I told myself that I would never lead a group of people the way this person did. I vowed to myself that I would always take responsibility and give credit while not forgetting to reflect before I coach my team members.

Internal Versus External Self-Awareness

All of us come with varying levels of self-awareness. You might find yourself to be more attuned to specific parts of yourself compared to other people. Well, there are two categories of self-awareness: external self-awareness and internal self-awareness. External self-awareness involves trying to understand how other people tend to view us. Every human being in this world comes with their own perspective of us depending on our goals and values. External self-awareness is something that can help you as a leader to develop a work environment where every member of your team will try to collaborate with each other.

Internal self-awareness is all about having loads of self-knowledge. All of us are well aware of our goals, feelings, passions, and values. You can acknowledge the weaknesses and strengths you have and try to make better decisions. It is something that would help you develop self-esteem and confidence and fix realistic goals for yourself.

Well, you might assume that internal self-awareness eliminates the need for external self-awareness or vice versa. You are wrong, my friend. Balance is the key here. You will have to make it a goal to balance your vision of yourself with the way in which other people see you. You cannot have internal self-awareness without the external version or have external self-awareness without the internal one.

SELF-CARE: A LEADER'S LIFELINE

Right before you start rolling your eyes and picture someone handing out yoga mats and spa vouchers, let me get one thing straight: Self-care has got nothing to do with heading to the mountaintop and chanting "om" as much as you can. I know it very well that you have a team to lead and to direct them toward success. Self-care can act like the backstage pass to your long-lasting leadership success.

Let us start with busting some myths. Self-care is not always about scented candles and bubble baths (don't get me wrong, they are nice as well). Self-care is about recharging your batteries intentionally so that you do not look like a zombie at the next team meeting. It involves acknowledging the fact that you are not a lifeless robot. In fact, the leaders who are the most resilient require a reboot. So what's in it for a leader like you?

To start with, self-care can help in enhancing your productivity. You can think of it like tuning a sports car—it might run just fine, but with a bit of tweaking, you can make it roar. When you are at the peak of your physical and mental condition after resting properly, you will get to make better decisions, inspire your team, and take care of curveballs just like a pro.

Reasons to Prioritize Self-Care

Self-care is a term that everyone knows about, but the overall concept is not much understood. It is never self-centered or selfish to focus on your well-being. Keep in mind that self-care is not a luxury. As you try to take care of yourself, you will get to feel positive, do your job as a leader in a better way, and help every member of your team to feel better as well. You can think of self-care as a way of demonstrating your respect for others and helping you bring your best self at work.

Self-care can be a win-win situation for you—your team will benefit and your organization too. But the thing is, although most leaders do understand the importance of self-care, they find it hard to know where to start. At times, it might be due to the fact that leaders have put others first for a long time that they have forgotten how to prioritize their own well-being in life. Other times, leaders get started with caring for themselves only after they experience burnout. You will have to understand that self-care can work best when you are proactive about it. The best thing about self-care is that it does not have to be time-consuming.

Here are some of the reasons why you need to prioritize self-care to be a better leader:

- *You get to set yourself up for a productive day*: The way in which you begin and end the day can affect your productivity to a great extent. When you create a daily morning routine, it will let you start each day with a positive attitude besides feeling more in control. The leaders I know or have spoken to like to read or work out, while others like to do some meditation. In the same way, a routine to end the day concentrating on relaxing activities can help in making you sleep better. The rituals will vary from one person to another. But what is more important here is to develop a routine that you know will work for you and make sure you stick to it.

- *You get to relate to the struggles of your team*: As you get to focus on self-care, you will accept all those areas of well-being that you are willing to improve. This, in turn, would let you be a more empathetic leader. You can turn into a leader who understands the struggles of the team members in a true sense. Being able to acknowledge your vulnerabilities can help the members of your team not just look up to you but also relate to you in a better way. Always keep in mind that team members would always trust a leader who is authentic by nature, someone who can very well admit their strengths and weaknesses.

- *You get to feel happiness, and it is transferable*: Self-care is one of the ways in which you get to regulate all your emotions besides being able to keep negative feelings in check. It is crucial as emotions can be contagious. Let me break this for you—people around you can easily pick up on your feelings, even across a computer screen. When you pay no attention to self-care and keep feeling stressed, exhausted, or frustrated, the members of your team will likely feel the same way. But when you can keep yourself energized and refreshed, your team members will absorb the positivity and apply it to their work and lives.

- *You get to be in touch with what is more important*: Do you know that concentrating on your well-being can help you focus on your core values? Yes, you heard me right. No individual in this world should concentrate on their work all the time. Besides being unhealthy for you, it is also an indication that you ignore your hobbies, friends, family, and all those priorities that create the person you truly are. Make time for self-care so that you can gain a new perspective and stay connected with yourself. It is all about ensuring that you have the energy and time for what truly matters to you apart from your work.

- *You get to make others invest in their well-being*: When you, as a leader, prioritize your psychological well-being and talk about it, it makes it easier for your entire team to do the same. It is exactly where authentic progress can actually start. It is quite important as the rate of burnout is on the rise now. Never feel scared or ashamed to share with your team how you are taking care of yourself and the ways it is helping you. You can provide them with a clear message regarding its importance.

- *You get to make better decisions*: Self-care is well-known for the mitigation of stress, which is vital for a leader. A bit of stress can pump up your adrenaline and make you ready for a critical meeting, but chronic stress might end up impacting your cognition and make things harder for you to make proper decisions. When you manage stress with the help of exercise or meditation, you start to think with a clear mind. Taking small breaks throughout the course of the day can also help in reducing stress.

Did you know that burnout can result in low morale and reduced productivity (Edú-Valsania et al., 2022)? I am sure getting to know about this will motivate you to focus on self-care. In fact, taking care of yourself allows you to focus on the problems of your team members (Klug et al., 2022).

Strategies of Self-Care

In order to be a great leader for other people, you will have to start taking care of yourself in the first place. Your team will always look to you for motivation and guidance in managing an organization. While employees may not always see how to start self-care from within, you, as a leader, can make them understand how self-care can be practiced and how it can help in running a team effectively.

Here are some strategies of self-care that can surely help you in your endeavor:

- *Setting boundaries*: It is the limit that you establish for how others should behave toward you including what you accept and what you do not. Setting boundaries is an essential form of self-care. It will make you identify what you require and ask for the same. Always try to be aware of your limits so that you can set up boundaries at work. Also, it would be of great help if you could state your boundaries in the right way, as it can help in avoiding confusion of all sorts. Make sure that you develop a proper schedule that aligns perfectly with your preferences.

- *Giving yourself grace*: When you are in a position of leadership, you might develop the feeling that you will need to solve everything right away. As you keep doing so, you might end up creating unrealistic expectations for yourself. You will have to provide yourself grace by being in control of your schedule. It would help in mitigating stress to a great extent. It would provide you with the time to understand how leadership is a lot more than taking all the burden on yourself. You will need to be flexible in the face of varying situations.

- *Extending grace to other people*: You will have to keep checking in with your team to find out how they face any crisis. You can ask your team members how they deal with problems. Keep this in mind, as showing interest in your team members can mean a lot to them.

CULTIVATING SELF-EMPATHY: THE UNSUNG HERO

Leadership can often feel like the entire weight of the world is on your shoulders, and everyone regards you as the workplace oracle. You have to deal with emails, meetings, and a to-do list that feels as stretched out as the Great Wall of China.

While being in the middle of all this chaos, have you ever paused for a moment and asked yourself, *Am I being too hard on myself?* Well, let me welcome you to the world of self-empathy, where you will turn yourself into the compassionate hero that you never thought you would need to be. No worries, as I will not ask you to talk to your reflection in the mirror (you can definitely do so if you feel like it). Self-empathy is similar to treating yourself in a way that you would treat your best friend who just dealt with a bad day—with understanding, kindness, and maybe a bucket of chocolate ice cream (you can go for any other flavor).

Let us start by getting a bit real here: Leaders can turn out to be their worst critics. In case your inner dialogue comprises phrases like, *I could have dealt with that in a better way* or *Why am I not able to deal with more tasks like Jane does?* self-empathy is right there knocking on your psychological door. Try to think about it—everyone expects you to have answers, be a mind reader at times, and make tough decisions, everything while trying to keep a smile on your face. It might seem like trying to run a marathon while juggling with knives (of course, metaphorically).

But what would happen if you could cut yourself some slack? Think of talking to your own self in a way that you would talk to a friend of yours who is in a more or less similar situation like you. Are you going to berate them for not being able to secure a project? I am sure your answer will be a "no." You would try to provide them with encouragement, right? Congrats! You have successfully decoded the secret handshake of self-empathy.

How can someone be the master of self-empathy? It would involve a bit of searching your soul and a willingness to get rid of all kinds of perfectionist tendencies. Here are some of the ways in which you can practice self-empathy:

- *Cultivating daily awareness*: Awareness is something that is well-known for driving change. You might end up missing various moments of life simply by not being able to savor the current moment. Self-awareness is often regarded as an essential component of self-empathy. Try to think of an email thread that is getting heated because of the reactive replies. What would happen if you took one step back and reread the emails after an hour? Could you decide whether a reply was required or not? It might be the case that the best course of action would be to arrange a call to address all kinds of misunderstandings. Keep in mind that you can always see any kind of situation with a new pair of eyes when you get to select responsive behaviors in place of reactive ones. You will have to provide yourself space and time to see things for what they truly are.

- *Celebrating small wins*: At times, it may feel like you are trying to push a boulder up the hill without even taking a break. So in order to deal with this feeling, try to take a moment and reflect on how you have overcome new challenges and embarked on new endeavors. You will have to do this on a daily basis. It might be the case where you were able to give the presentation you were feeling scared of with superb confidence or have that tough conversation you were trying to avoid. The aim here is to make you understand that it is necessary to celebrate small wins. You will keep navigating the valleys and peaks of life, but nothing will make sense unless you get to celebrate your victories, even the minute ones.

- *Creating space for connection and dialogue*: You will have to replace your tendency of rumination with a healthy form of self-dialogue. It involves establishing a connection with your own self. For all those repetitive thoughts that do not tend to be supportive in any way, you will have to reframe them for the development of a new mindset. You will have to focus on compassionate inner dialogue. For instance, if you keep thinking, *Nothing I do can be considered good as a leader*, you can change this to, *I did the best I could today. I will try to do even better tomorrow.*

- *Getting rid of perfectionism*: A huge part of self-empathy is not trying to do everything. You will have to let yourself ask for help whenever you require it. It could be the case that the workload you are taking care of is not balanced, and you might require more support to deliver the expected outcome. Or you might require additional support in your journey as a leader. Keep in mind that there is no shame in seeking the help of a coach or a therapist, or reading books to help yourself on the journey. In case you are aware of the areas where additional support would help, seek out what you require. There is no need to be perfect. Perfectionism is what gives rise to monotony in life.

- *Controlling what is in your control*: The only thing that you can control all the time is your inner state. As a leader, you can try to be more centered in dealing with the storms that your team might have to go through. All I mean here is understanding and accepting what is truly under your control as a leader. Doing so would help in eliminating the tendency to shame and blame your own self.

BUILDING A SELF-CARE ROUTINE: PRACTICAL STEPS

Hey fearless leaders! I can see you trying to juggle tasks just like a circus performer while trying your best to lead your entire team to victory. However, here is the thing—even superheroes need a day off from saving the world.

Welcome to the world of self-care, where you will take care of yourself without any need to wear a cape (you can definitely wear it if that is your thing). You might think, *Self-care? I don't have time for bubble baths as I have got deadlines to meet.* Well, as already said earlier, self-care is not only about taking bubble baths.

Practicing Self-Care

Here are some of the ways in which you can start practicing self-care:

- *Refueling and re-energizing*: Hard work can turn out to be both physically and mentally tiring. In order to make sure that you keep performing with maximum potential, it is necessary to make time during the course of the day to refuel and re-energize. A great way to reduce stress is breathing exercises. Every human being breathes in a different way when relaxed in comparison to when they are stressed. Strained breathing is short and quick, whereas natural breathing is deep and slow. Simply by taking out a bit of time from your routine to concentrate on your breathing, you can easily kick out stress from your life. Another superb way to re-energize yourself is to include small bits of joy into your everyday schedule. For instance, if you feel happy when you listen to music, you can set aside 10 minutes every day to just sit back and listen to your favorite music in peace.

- *Practicing kindness*: It might seem obvious, but even a small bit of kindness can actually go a long way. Trying to run a successful organization is not an easy job, but it is easy to allow stress to direct your mood. In order to be a great leader, it is necessary to put aside any kind of negativity that you might be feeling and remember to be kind to your team members and also yourself. It has been found that there lies a direct link between success and kindness (McQuaid, 2018). As you try to balance out self-care and kindness, let kindness guide all your interactions.

- *Taking time to reflect every day*: At times, when we come across the term *self-care*, all that we can focus on is to put away work from our minds completely. There is no doubt that it is an effective strategy, but trying to think about work in a different light can also turn out to be quite effective. In order to maintain a positive mindset, try to take some moment to reflect at the end of every day. Right as you get done with your day, try to think of everything that took place during the day, the stressors you faced, and the lessons you learned. Simply by changing a stressful situation into a learning experience, you can easily start seeing things through an actionable frame of reference. When you have a greater perspective, you can react to the same kind of event without making yourself go through the same kind of stress.

- *Being aware of your internal voice*: All of us have got an internal voice that keeps speaking to us the entire day. The voice is capable enough of making various tones. The tone that your internal voice takes is dependent on the kind of attitude you hold. In case you find your internal voice to be judgmental and negative, you will have to take necessary steps to change it. You will have to find out what your voice is trying to say and, where it is coming from and respond to it accordingly. The internal voice can say a lot regarding the way you feel, and it is necessary to be aware of when the voice tends to take a harsh tone.

- *Practicing self-affirmations every day*: Not every human being can form positive thoughts about themselves automatically. If you struggle to be complementary and tend to judge harshly, you will have to look out for ways in which you can enhance your self-worth. Every morning, as you wake up, start the day with self-affirmations. I am not saying that you will have to stand in front of the mirror and try to talk to yourself. All you have to do is take a few minutes to think about the positive traits you possess and how well you will do that day. You will have to speak positive thoughts into existence.

- *Connecting with nature*: Trying to find some time to connect with nature is a superb way of self-care. It is said that spending some time in nature can turn out to be therapeutic. When you stay outdoors, you will get to remove yourself from the hustle and bustle of work life and let yourself have a look at the bigger picture. You can get to realize what life is all about. No matter if you use a portion of your leisure time to take a walk in the park or to go on a hike, spending about an hour can turn out to be a calming exercise.

Give your best to make self-care more like a habit. Similar to brushing your teeth every morning or checking your emails, self-care and self-empathy needs to be non-negotiable. You will have to schedule them into your calendar and treat them like a VIP guest whom you cannot cancel. Keep calm and prioritize self-care!

Publishing.com
helped create and
publish this book.

As a self publisher, I would like to thank
Publishing.com for their professional assistance
with publishing this book.

Publishing has changed my life, and I would like
to empower my readers with the same
opportunity to reach your dreams, start a side
hustle and earn extra income.

No writing skills required!

Scan this!

**JOIN AT
MYPUBLISHING.COM/PATHWAYSPRESS-LWE
TODAY AND MAKE PASSIVE INCOME PUBLISHING**

CHAPTER 3:
MAKING EMPATHY ACTIONABLE—EVERYDAY LEADERSHIP PRACTICES

I'll be damned if I am not getting tired of this. It seems to be the profession of a President simply to hear other people talk.
—William Howard Taft

Have you ever come across those moments when leadership felt like those fancy titles, wearing suits that are a bit tight, and boardroom speeches? Well, buckle up to get your mind blown, and not only by the waistband of your attire. Leadership is not about flying around the workplace with a superhero cape or being able to give motivational speeches that are better than TED Talks. Leadership is more like a daily gig, like the person who can easily fix the office printer or the unofficial coffee expert at the office.

In the roller-coaster ride of leadership, I am going to uncover all those hidden gems of leadership that most leaders tend to overlook while reaching for the last slice of pizza in the break room. Let me tell you that it is not about being the person with the ancient job title or the loudest person in the room. It is about the subtle and small things that you do that tend to make a world of difference.

We will dive into the art of active listening (no, it does not involve nodding your head while making plans for the weekend in mind), the power of asking questions, and the art of giving and receiving feedback. So let's get started!

ACTIVE LISTENING:
THE HEARTBEAT OF EMPATHETIC COMMUNICATION

Listening can be regarded as one of the core skills of communication. It is something that is necessary for proper leadership. Active listening is important for team performance. When a leader turns out to be judgmental, it can make the team members afraid of them, besides not having the willingness to communicate.

Try to think of this—you are in a meeting where everyone is trying to present their views at once. It might seem like a chaotic symphony, and you are the leader who is trying to make sense of it all. Do you know what can help you here? Yes, you guessed it right—active listening. It can turn out to be your magic baton.

Active listening is not only about listening to the words that are being spoken. It also involves trying to read between the lines, trying to understand what is unsaid, and also decoding the emotional side. Active listening is more like a spy mission. You will not only be hearing what is being said; you will also have to decode the hidden messages. Is Steven from IT terrified about the new project? Or is Sandra from HR doing jazz hands to showcase her enthusiasm for the new project? Well, it is your duty to find out.

Importance of Active Listening as a Leader

Why are listening skills crucial? Here are some of the ways in which listening skills can make you a better leader:

- *It can enhance your capacity as a leader*: It is always possible to learn something new from people around you. By people, I also mean your team members. Active listening can provide you with perspective and knowledge that can directly help in enhancing your capacity for leadership. When you are open to new ideas and feedback from your team members, it can help you grow as a leader.

- *It helps in comprehending the situation*: In case you cannot pay attention to what is being said by your team members, you can never get to understand any situation in a true sense. When you fail to comprehend a situation, it might make you give recommendations or advice that are not effective, or you might not be able to get to the root of issues.

- *It will show that you care*: When you truly listen to someone, it will show that you care for what is being said and also empathize with what they feel. It can help in the creation of a trustable work environment. When your team members can trust you, it will provide you with more influence over them. Additionally, it can motivate them more and will also make them committed to their work.

- *It can provide you with a vision of reality*: It is necessary to have insights and knowledge about the everyday reality of all your team members. Listening can provide you with this ability. It is important to develop an atmosphere that is filled with trust, an environment that can encourage the members of your team to speak up about their everyday challenges. I am sure you will be surprised at how different their reality is from what you think it to be.

Challenges of Active Listening

You can think of active listening as a skill, an art, and a discipline that also involves some great degree of self-control. In order to develop proper listening skills, you will have to get an idea of all those things that are involved in effective communication and cultivate the skills to sit down and listen quietly. It would involve not paying attention to any of your requirements and concentrating on the person who is speaking.

It is a task that is made even more difficult by how our brains function. When a person talks to you, your brain will start processing the words instantly, along with the tone, body language, and perceived meanings that are coming from the speaker. In place of hearing one noise, you actually hear two: the noise that is made by the other person and the one in your own mind. Unless you can train your mind to stay vigilant, you will end up focusing on the noise that is running in your head. It is exactly where techniques of active listening come into play.

Hearing can be transformed into listening only when you focus on what is being said by the other person and also follow the same closely. In order to do this, you will have to be aware of which of the noises you are listening to and redirect your lost attention back to the person who is speaking the moment you get off the track.

Honing Active Listening Skills as a Leader

Here are some of the ways in which you can be an active listener and lead your team in a better way:

- *Concentrating on the person and the message*: You will have to direct all your attention to the speaker and listen without any kind of judgment. Also, you will have to try not to formulate any response midway as they speak. Focus on the body language of the speaker and also their words. It could turn out to be the hardest step of all, as most of us are used to paying attention to the noise in our minds.

- *Being fully present*: Learning to listen actively would require patience, presence, and practice. As a leader, it demonstrates your interest in the views of others, builds trust, and deepens your understanding of your entire team, various situations, and problems. All you have to do is quiet your mind while getting rid of the desire to fix and release all your judgments.

- *Communicating attention*: Anyone can tell when you are not focusing or paying attention. So you will have to utilize your gestures and body language to make them aware that you are absolutely aligned with what is being said. Some easy active listening exercises would be to face the speaker directly and maintain eye contact, stand or sit in an open position, and nod or smile occasionally.

- *Not responding in the moment*: One of the best ways of practicing active listening is not to respond in the moment. Simply try to take in all that you can hear, thank people for all their thoughts, and inform them that you would like to take some days to reply to their input. Next, you will have to fix a follow-up time so that you get to close the loop on what your team members are thinking.

- *Acknowledging what is being said*: Try to interject with something like, "I see," or, "Uh-huh," from time to time in order to indicate that you are truly following what is being said. Such acknowledgment does not indicate that you agree with the individual. All it indicates is that you are listening actively. In fact, it is a great technique to keep all the attention focused on the other person and also the message instead of the noise that you tend to hear in your head.

- *Practicing humility*: You will have to try and practice the phrase, "All that I can hear you saying is [state the concern]. Is there anything that I am missing or getting it wrong?" Such a phrase could help you extract key insights as a leader. This would need humility in the first place, to have the belief that you might not have understood something, and then trusting that there might be more in store that would be worth knowing about. Such a combination of listening and humility is important if you are willing to make a high-performing team.

- *Stop interrupting*: It could be a hard thing to do as your brain would always want to jump in and get a solution for the issue before it has been communicated by the speaker. When you try to interrupt someone as they speak, it showcases disrespect and impatience. It is specifically the case when you end up interrupting with an argument instead of a question. It can easily frustrate a speaker and will end up limiting your overall understanding of the message. Active listening is all about having patience and letting the speaker finish every point before you can ask more questions. Interruption will not let you get a complete hold of a situation.

Being an active listener is something that would require both training and patience. It is not about stopping yourself from interjecting and holding the opinions you have until the speaker is done. It is about trying to consider all those things that are being said before you can respond to them.

I believe that a great meeting is when your opinion regarding something gets changed. That will not happen unless you can be an active listener. I have gained the majority of my active listening skills while working on my marriage. If I care so much about the person I am married to, I should do my best to listen to what they have to say, take into consideration their comments, and then respond.

And what about the people I lead? The members of my team have chosen me as their leader. The very least I can do is provide them with the opportunity to be heard and considered.

EMPATHETIC COMMUNICATION: MORE THAN JUST WORDS

Do you know that communication extends to more than just words? Yes, you heard me right. How you say it and the body language that you hold while saying something can make a great deal of difference. It is extremely important to pay attention to your body language as you speak to your team members, as it helps in sending out nonverbal cues that might easily undermine all that is being said.

When your title starts getting bigger, you are most likely to get removed from people and also the general workings of the workplace. People are most likely to see you less. So when you meet with your team, the way you move your hands and body and what you do with your eyes can make a huge impact.

Let me share a quick fact with you—the tone of your voice can easily convey a lot more meaning than what you say. It has also been found that around 38% of communication is about tone and voice, 55% is about body language, and only the remaining 7% is about the words that you speak (The British Library, n.d.).

Empathetic communication is important for effective communication, just like caffeine is necessary to get started on Monday mornings. I know what you might be thinking, *Seriously? Now we will have to learn about how I pitch my voice and wave my hands?* Yes, whether you believe me or not, your vocal cords and body are the secret weapons of empathy. You can think of them as the Robin and Batman of the leadership game, but no worries, as it involves a lot less mask and cape action (just kidding).

So here are some of the ways in which you can practice empathetic communication with your team members.

Deciding What to Convey

Everything that you do, like the way you talk, walk, look at others, gesture, sit down, and more, communicates something about who you are. So the most important step that you will have to consider as a leader is, *Who is the 'I' that I try to present in front of my team members? Can I successfully convey all those qualities that I want?* You will have to adopt a kind of body language that is in sync with your behavior and something that can define the kind of leader you wish to be.

Sitting Next to Team Members

Try to change the shape of the meeting tables from rectangular to circular. But in case that is not possible and you will have to work with the rectangular ones, try not to sit at the head of the table. Also, do not try to run meetings all by yourself all the time. Try to sit next to your team members that would show you are one of them. Rotate the responsibility of heading meetings, and then take part as if you are also a member of the team. This can be seen as one of the strongest forms of body language—being fully engaged with the team instead of standing apart.

Empathetic Mannerisms

It is possible to communicate empathy by being fully present with the team, maintaining soft and attentive eye contact, keeping your shoulders squared, having your arms by your side, and nodding your head when your team members express themselves. If you need to respond, try to reflect back on what the members of your team have said.

Balancing Between Closed and Open Body Language

Having too much open body language or showing eagerness with your body language might end up making your team members uncomfortable. For example, while holding a power pose might make you look more confident as a leader, in certain cases, it might be perceived as arrogance. In case you are too closed off, it can make your team members feel that you do not even care. For instance, leaders who tend to keep their heads down are regarded as doubtful. The best thing that you can do here is to relax and be conscious of the message that you send with your body language. Find the midpoint between closed and open body language.

Eye Contact to Build Trust

Nothing could be more important than eye contact. Trying to look directly into the eyes of your team members and listening to what they say (without the intention of answering immediately) can help in the development of trust between you as a leader and your team members. When you tend to look around and do not focus on the team, you may come across as insincere or distracted. This can hamper trust.

Mirroring the Body Language of Others

As you speak to a group, do your best to open yourself up. Keep your arms relaxed with your shoulders back. You can use your hands to gesture toward yourself and your team as if you are trying to connect the two. When you have one-on-one conversations, mirror or match the tone and body language of the other person, as it would help in developing a bond of trust naturally.

EMPATHY IN DECISION-MAKING: BALANCING LOGIC AND EMOTION

Try to think of this—you will have to make a decision that could either make your team experience new success or make them feel as if they are on a sinking ship. It is in moments of this sort that empathy jumps into the scene, all ready to save your day. I am not suggesting having a group cry session whenever you need to make a tough decision. Using empathy in decision-making will act as the secret decoder ring that will help you understand how the decision you make will ripple through the minds and hearts of the team. It involves being able to read between the lines and making all those choices that would not only make sense on paper but would also be effective in real life.

As a leader, you will have to consider the inputs of your team members and also the personal and emotional impacts on them. You will have to ask for team input and also communicate all kinds of decisions with understanding and transparency.

Here are the steps that you can follow to make decisions with empathy:

- *Determining the issue*: You will have to identify the decision by considering the issue, the way it looks at the moment, and how you would want it to look later. You can also ask yourself, *Who is getting affected negatively because of the problem?*

- *Gathering information*: When you try to research the problem, use all kinds of hard data that you have and also your own observations. You can ask your team members, "How does the problem affect your position and yourself?"

- *Identifying possible solutions*: The majority of decisions will be a lot more than a "this or that" kind of choice. So you will need to work toward finding all the possible solutions along with your team. Discuss with your team what will be the negative and positive impacts of each of the choices.

- *Evaluating options*: Every solution that you find will come with pros and cons for the people involved and also for the organization. You will have to understand that some people will get hit harder by the decision compared to other people. You can ask yourself, *Are there any possible ways in which the negative impact of the choice can be minimized?* Do not forget to ask the same to your team members.

- *Making decision*: No matter what you decide, always think about how the implementation of the decision will change the expectations and requirements of all the people who are involved. At times, you might be able to make a decision by completing either one of these steps or after completing all of them. Keep in mind that there will be times when the process of making a decision will turn out to be more difficult as you keep discovering things throughout the process.

Try to understand the people who are involved, their hopes, concerns, and what they expect from you as a leader. It is all about understanding that decisions are not always about figures and facts; they are about the people who will be affected by those figures and facts.

CHAPTER 4:
BUILDING BRIDGES—EMPATHY AND CULTURAL SENSITIVITY IN DIVERSE TEAMS

Diversity is the one true thing we all have in common. Celebrate it every day. –Winston Churchill

Let me welcome you all to the world of cultural diversity in your team. You might think, *Why should someone care about diversity in their team? Why can't I just simply get the job done?* Well, hold onto your leadership hat as we embark on a journey that will surely change how you see your team.

Try to think of your team as a kaleidoscope. Every member of your team resembles a unique and colorful piece of glass. As you try to shake the kaleidoscope, the glass pieces come together and create ever-changing and beautiful patterns. You can think of this as diversity in action. It is not at all a buzzword. It is like a secret sauce that can easily make your team sparkle.

Now you might be wondering, *What is the importance of this?* Just think about it. Would you ever want a team where every individual acts, talks, and thinks in the same way? That is going to be as exciting as a monochromatic movie. You have to understand that diversity can add spice to work life. It can help in bringing new perspectives, ideas, and a great deal of creativity right to the table.

But keep in mind that managing a diverse team is never going to be easy. It will not be smooth sailing all the time. Do not worry, as I am here to help. In this section, we will develop the foundation to understand the cultural kaleidoscope within your team.

THE CULTURAL KALEIDOSCOPE: UNDERSTANDING THE DIVERSITY OF YOUR TEAM

Diversity in the workplace is about employing people of different cultures, genders, ages, and educational backgrounds. Not only is diversity important for social justice and creativity but it has also been found that companies with diverse teams can experience greater financial returns compared to companies that are not very diverse (Hunt et al., 2015).

When you have a diverse team, you will find unique solutions and make proper decisions. When you are aware of how such a team can benefit the workplace, you will be able to hire individuals with distinct skills and backgrounds. So in simple terms, a diverse team is a group of people who come together with different skills and backgrounds and work as a team to attain specific goals. You, as a leader, will have to take care of team diversity. Are you aware of the benefits of a diverse team? Let's have a look at them.

Better Innovation and Creativity

When you craft a team with varied backgrounds, thoughts, and inputs, you can find creative ways to solve issues. It is primarily because every member of the team will come to the table with different ideas and perspectives.

Improved Problem-Solving

A team that can create and find innovative solutions can easily make informed decisions. It would help in faster problem-solving besides offering solutions that would benefit company performance. Also, teams can analyze information and data carefully before they get to make decisions that would impact the overall company.

Better Employee Engagement

Diverse teams permit individuals to participate actively and also share the ideas they have got. This can lead to better engagement and performance across the team you lead. It is primarily because every member of the team will feel more motivated to attain the goals of the company.

HARNESSING EMPATHY TO NAVIGATE CULTURAL NUANCES

Trying to lead a diverse team might feel like conducting a symphony, and that too in a foreign language. There is nothing to worry about as we have an empathy baton for conducting this orchestra.

There are leaders who can now lead diversified teams very well and also take care of the challenges that come along with cross-cultural management. I am talking about different motivational factors and communication styles. The easiest way to deal with such hurdles is to try and lead with cross-cultural empathy. It is something that would encourage you to be curious to get to know new things from one another, to be mindful regarding the way we communicate, and also to check in with our assumptions as we settle conflicts.

It is crucial for modern-day leaders to cultivate the art of cultural intelligence. It is nothing but the simple ability to relate to and connect with people coming from different cultures. A great starting point as a leader is to be more culturally sensitive by truly being willing to learn about the cultures of your team members.

Adapting to Different Styles of Communication

You must have come across team members who prefer to be direct with what they say regarding their thoughts. No matter the communication style that you encounter, you will have to prevent yourself from falling into the trap of thinking that there should only be a way of getting done with things and simply dismissing any other alternative solution. As an empathetic leader, you will have to listen to understand and not only to reply. As you do so, you will get to understand the thought process of your team members and then make decisions.

Checking In With Your Assumptions

At times, conflict might turn out to be inevitable. So what can be done here? In a situation where conflict arises, the chances are high that you might have filtered information using your own cultural lens. You might not be able to understand this, but it could be the primary source of the misunderstanding. In such an instance, it would help if you could move a step back and check your assumptions by providing particular feedback on the behavior you observe and asking for clarification. As you check your assumptions, you will get to acknowledge that your biases might have been contributing to the friction in how your team is performing.

Excelling at Empathy

One of the best ways to build cultural self-awareness as a leader is to keep interacting with people from different cultures. All those leaders who tend to demonstrate empathy with the members of their team can easily bridge all kinds of cultural differences. Such leaders can excel at leading diverse cultural teams besides being able to connect with customers all over the globe.

INCLUSIVE LEADERSHIP: FOSTERING A CULTURE THAT VALUES DIVERSITY

Diversity, inclusion, and equity can be regarded as the foundational aspects of the overall growth and performance of an organization, especially in today's world. But as workplaces adapt to modern culture, specifically when there is an increase in hybrid work setups, development, and maintenance of an inclusive work environment have turned out to be a true challenge. In order to take care of this challenge of inclusivity, you will have to turn into an inclusive leader.

Inclusive leadership is a style of leadership that concentrates on leading a group of team members while showcasing true respect for their uniqueness and individuality. It gets characterized by empathy and also a commitment not to focus on biases. Moreover, inclusive leaders would never discriminate based on certain factors like color, race, or other characteristics. In place of doing so, they try to create a work environment where every team member gets to feel valued for their perspectives and unique contributions.

Inclusive Leadership and Its Importance

Did you know that teams led by inclusive leaders are 17% more likely to showcase higher performance (Bourke & Titus, 2019)? I know you might be shocked by this, but this is true. In fact, you can check it out yourself once you turn yourself into an inclusive leader. Want to know why inclusive leadership is so important, especially in today's world? Let me share it with you.

- Leadership style of this sort can help a lot with team dynamics besides improving communication.
- It can help in fostering collaboration and teamwork.
- You can make sure that all team members feel respected and valued.
- It helps in boosting employee efficiency and productivity.
- It can help in yielding improved work quality and high job satisfaction.

How to Foster Equality and Diversity Within Your Team

Here are some of the ways in which you can foster diversity and equality within your team:

- *Being aware of unconscious bias*: An individual who is in the role of leadership needs to acknowledge and understand their unconscious bias. You can think of it as the foundation of developing an equal, diverse, and inclusive workplace. It does not matter how inclusive a person believes they are; unconscious biases can be found in all of us. Try to engage in self-reflection and also work on such biases. Also, try to depend on data and facts as you make decisions to stop yourself from being influenced by biases.
- *Promoting practices of inclusive hiring*: Ensure that the process of recruitment is fair and inclusive. This can be done by seeking employees from various backgrounds.

- *Encouraging open communication*: You are the one who will have to promote a safe place for all your employees where they can communicate comfortably and get to share their experiences and perspectives.
- *Encouraging feedback*: Asking for feedback is one of the best ways to better understand the challenges and requirements of the team. It can also help in the reduction of discrimination and bias within an organization.

Challenges of Inclusive Leadership

There are certain challenges of inclusive leadership that you should know about. Let's have a look at them:

- *Resistance to change*: In today's workplace, change is present all the time. But when it comes to the promotion of diversity and inclusivity, inclusive leadership might come across one of the most challenging hurdles, and that is change. It is true that change can result in great success, but not every individual in an organization can embrace it. It is mainly because change might also bring stress, anxiety, and fear to many. But how can a leader overcome this? Start by fostering an environment that embraces constant improvement and innovation. Also, try to offer employee training to help in navigating the changes.
- *Workplace tensions and conflicts*: Bringing together a team with diverse experiences and perspectives can

surely result in misunderstandings, disagreements, and personal grievances. But only because it might be challenging—it does not indicate that leaders should stay away from inclusion and diversity. In fact, inclusivity is something that might lead to superb results and foster growth within the organization and team. Try to stay away from assumptions and focus on perspectives from various sources. Define responsibilities, roles, and goals for the reduction of potential conflicts and misunderstandings.

Best Practices for the Cultivation of an Inclusive Workplace Culture

Let's have a look at some of the practices that can help in the cultivation of an inclusive workplace culture:

- Workplace inclusivity is something that always starts with leaders. So leaders need to demonstrate a commitment to inclusion and diversity.
- Conduct inclusion and diversity training on a daily basis to enhance employee awareness and understanding.
- Encourage diverse recruitment strategies within the workplace so that you do not end up missing out on exceptional employees. You can also practice blind interviews for the reduction of biases.
- As a leader, connect with the members of your team on a personal level and allow them to talk to you freely without any kind of repercussions.

- Involve team members from various backgrounds in decision-making to make sure various kinds of perspectives get considered.
- Lead by example. Keep in mind that inclusive leadership can always help in fostering a healthy work environment.

My first experience of working on a diverse team was as an overnight team leader at Target when I was quite young. It was situated in Frisco, Texas. I worked with a team of exclusively Spanish-speaking team members. I had learned Spanish in school (from middle school through college) but was required to only speak Spanish at work.

While working at Target, I got to learn so much about this group of super hard-working people that was previously unknown to me. After some time, I got included in the group, having lunch together, staying late to help each other out, and joking around. The feeling that I had of being lonely and on my own was replaced with a feeling of acceptance and friendship. I wanted to be able to foster that later on in my career.

Throughout my career, I've been conscientious when interviewing, not judging an individual on anything other than their merit. Where I saw this happening a lot in my career was through age discrimination or age bias. I recall having an interview with someone for a role while I was at King of Pops. I was overwhelmed by the story and experience of the woman who I was interviewing (her name was Beth). She went through an incredible resume of all of her experiences and then just leveled with me. She said, "Pete, give me a chance to prove myself. No one will because of my age. I know I am overqualified, but that's the excuse everyone has given me when they reject me for a job."

Looking back, Beth was one of my best producers, and it taught me a truly valuable lesson: give a chance to people who have been "written off" by others. These people will appreciate the opportunity and work harder than those who have been handed a role. Since then, I have used the same mindset when building new teams and task forces. I have intentionally included members from the team of all levels of experience and tenure.

As you start nurturing inclusive leadership within your team and organization, the results will surely make you mesmerized. Moreover, you will get to develop a work culture where bias has no place.

CHAPTER 5:
NAVIGATING THE VIRTUAL LANDSCAPE—
EMPATHY IN REMOTE LEADERSHIP

Leadership is the art of getting someone else to do something you want done because he wants to do it. –Dwight D. Eisenhower

The age of remote work—an era where we feel like living in little bubbles—is all connected by the wonders of the internet. The new world of remote work has also brought with it a new approach to leadership. Here's a quick fact for you—about 56% of the U.S. workforce holds a job that is compatible with the concept of remote work (Global Workplace Analytics, n.d.).

Did you know what the secret sauce of remote work leadership is? Yes, yes, you guessed it right. Empathy. In the past years, leadership was primarily about being the boss, someone who could keep giving out orders and maybe delivering one or two motivational speeches at times. But in the present scenario, with team members scattered all over the world just like confetti at a party, things are bound to change.

Enter empathy. It can be regarded as the secret power in the world of remote work. In place of barking orders, leaders are required to ask, "How are you all feeling today? Is there anything that I can do to help?" It is about understanding that a member of your team might be dealing with a dog who thinks the work desk is a comfy bed or a toddler who has made up their mind that conference calls are the best time to practice their great dance moves.

Empathy can be regarded as the Swiss Army knife that is meant for leaders. It is not only about providing a shoulder to cry on when things turn out to be bitter (virtual tissues are appreciated all the time). It also involves understanding the unique hardships that every member of your team has to go through in their remote work. Maybe Brian from accounting has a Wi-Fi connection that is as slow as a snail. Or Mary from marketing is trying to juggle work while taking care of her two kids. Empathy is something that can help you see their world right through their webcam.

Here is the best thing: As you try to lead your team with empathy, you will not only be creating fuzzy and warm feelings. You will also build connected, strong, and productive teams. When every member of your team knows that you have got their back, they will be willing to move mountains to get the job done. So as we start navigating the new world of remote work, keep in mind that empathy is the secret weapon that you have. You will have to be the leader who listens and understands.

EMBRACING THE REMOTE WORK REVOLUTION

Empathy is important in any kind of workplace. However, it turns out to be even more important when it comes to remote work. People who work remotely are bound to feel disconnected from the entire team, which might result in feelings of disengagement, loneliness, and depression. Empathy can readily help in creating a sense of belonging and community, which can directly enhance job satisfaction, employee engagement, and overall well-being. Do you know that empathy can help in developing trust between the members of a team? When employees feel that their coworkers can understand their feelings and value the perspectives they hold, they will be more likely to share their opinions and ideas.

Empathy and Its Role on Remote Teams

By now, you must have understood that, as a leader, empathy is about connecting with the members of your team trying to acknowledge all their emotions besides understanding their circumstances. There are people who really love to say that their organization is like their extended family. However, most organizations fail to create a culture of empathy, mutual trust, and respect among team members. Here are some of the ways in which you can practice empathy while leading remote teams:

- *Practicing listening skills*: Being able to understand what team members have got to say regarding what they feel and, most importantly, what they fail to say, in place of giving out generic advice, can help in the creation of an empathetic environment in a remote work setting. To permit better inclusivity, it is necessary for a leader to try and see things from different perspectives. Nothing can be better than encouraging your team members to opt for meaningful conversations with you. On your part, you will have to listen to them with empathy and enthusiasm.

- *Not being harsh*: Trying to work and communicate remotely with the help of virtual platforms while struggling to maintain the expected productivity can turn out to be quite challenging. Holding a resolute stance is necessary if a team member lacks productivity, but this does not indicate that you will opt for strict or harsh responses. What I have found is that trying to cultivate a culture of reasoning with your team members, followed by understanding their point of view, can be pretty effective.

- *Making it a safe space to request help*: Asking for help, especially in a virtual setting, can be a hard thing to do. As a leader, you will have to offer help to the members of your team at every opportunity. You will have to show others that it is completely okay to request help by doing it yourself. No one can inspire a team other than the person who leads it, and that is you. When you ask for help, you can make others feel that it is safe to do the same.

- *Increasing recognition*: People who work remotely and in isolation might feel underappreciated. So it is necessary for you to enhance your efforts of recognition to make sure that everyone in your team can feel that what they do for the organization is valued. Keep in mind that employee recognition is not required to be expensive. At times, simple acts like offering development opportunities, acknowledging someone in meetings, or small tokens of appreciation can do a lot in making someone feel special and valued.

Monitoring Empathy in Remote Work Setting

Trying to monitor empathy in a remote work setting can turn out to be a true challenge. This is primarily because there will be fewer chances for direct face-to-face interactions. But there are certain strategies that can surely help in the promotion of empathy. The first thing that you will have to do is develop clear channels of communication that would allow remote workers to connect with the team members. It could involve instant messaging, video calls, and email. You will have to encourage the members of your team to share all their challenges, issues, experiences, and successes. It is also necessary to provide resources and training that would allow remote workers to develop their skills of empathy. This might involve coaching, participating in online courses, and mentoring.

Remote work is a big thing now for me. I am the COO of Publishing.com, which is a fully remote worldwide company. We have to leverage Slack and maximize communication in order to nurture a strong and thriving culture. Additionally, we empower our team members and not micromanage them. However, we have to hold people accountable through results. Want to travel to Barbados for the week for work? Sure, no problem, but you need to get your work done and done well. Remote work is the future of the landscape, and allowing your team to work remotely when possible provides an incredible win for their personal lives.

BUILDING CONNECTIONS IN A VIRTUAL ENVIRONMENT

With the advent of the remote work culture, building connections has gained more importance. If you work with your team in a physical environment, you can interact with each other face-to-face, share ideas, celebrate small wins, and so on. But when it comes to remote work, doing such things might be challenging. No worries, as I am here to help you out.

Here are some of the ways in which you can build connections in a remote work environment.

Determine the Right Tools

You will have to find out the correct tools for all your remote work communications. Never try to fit a workplace into a communication tool. It is important to develop an environment that would make sure that all team members can feel safe and also empowered to share all their ideas and thoughts. The aim is to foster a team culture that is collaborative in nature. So try to find communication tools that would suit the environment of your organization in the best possible way. I am sure most of them would go beyond simple video conferencing.

Conduct Video Meetings

Video conferences or meetings are the best thing when it is not possible to communicate face-to-face. Video calls would permit you and the members of your team to see one another. It could help in the replication of in-person interaction.

There are various tools that you can use for the purpose of video conferencing, like Skype and Zoom. Try to set up video meetings, and you can also encourage managers who work under you to do the same. Are you worried about the mess of your home office? No worries, as there are video conferencing tools that would let you change the video background. Good luck with interacting with your whole team right on a Caribbean beach!

Celebrate!

As you stop meeting in person, it is quite easy to stop celebrating all those things that you would generally celebrate when in the office, such as holidays or birthdays. Never allow the virtual world to stop you and your team from celebrating the little joys of the workplace. Is a member of your team having a baby? Why not celebrate a virtual baby shower? You can ask all the members of your team to wear blue or pink in honor of the little life. Or is someone in your team having their birthday? Try having a party! Sing "Happy Birthday" on video calls or have your team members comment on a virtual birthday card. Just cracked a new project? Celebrate online with your whole team. Just because you are not meeting in person does not indicate that you cannot have fun events.

Conduct Daily Check-Ins

Everyday check-ins that involve every member of the team can turn out to be helpful in keeping your team members connected and motivated. Provide opportunities for your employees to recognize each other for good work, discuss the values of the company, and as said in the last point, do not forget to have fun. Conduct silly quizzes sometimes, or you can also watch a TED Talks video with the whole team and have a discussion session.

Share Photos

Sharing photos is a superb way in which you can bring a personal touch to the days of your team members. You can have a virtual week every month. You will have to set a different theme every day. For instance, you can set one day as a "happy place day" where everyone will upload and share photos of their happy place and also explain why it is their happy place.

Or you can set one day as a "pet day" and encourage everyone to share photos of their pets. The photos can be shared via email or on a shared drive, whatever suits best for your remote work setup. Sharing photos can readily help in emphasizing the human connection that a remote team might miss out on.

Acknowledge Accomplishments

It might be something that you have been doing prior to transitioning to a remote work environment. However, in a remote work setup, it is even more important. Ensure that you acknowledge all the accomplishments of your team members, not only to them but also to their fellow teammates too. As you do so, it will show that you are truly proud of the members of your team and value their contribution to the workplace. You can do so in various ways, like through phone calls, via recognition emails, or by including them in a team newsletter.

EMPATHY IN COMMUNICATION:
THE ART OF VIRTUAL CONVERSATIONS

How can someone forget the joys of remote work: You can skip the commute, stay away from the office coffee that fails to energize you, and best of all, you get to attend meetings in boxers or pajamas (don't forget to wear a professional-looking shirt or T-shirt above; just kidding). However, let us try to get real for a moment. Effective communication in the virtual space could feel like trying to find the piece of sock that disappears in the laundry basket all the time—it is tricky but important. So how can someone be a communication maestro in the virtual world?

To start with, we have got video calls. They have turned out to be a staple of remote work. It is true that video calls are really useful, but they also come with their own quirks. I am sure you know what I am trying to talk about: the awkward pauses, frozen faces, and also the accidental mute moments that can make others feel like you are giving a silent monologue. To avoid all of these, you will have to promote the three Ps—preparation, patience, and a dash of paprika.

Let me break the Ps for you. Preparation is about ensuring that the Wi-Fi is working fine and the background is not a mountain of laundry that is all set to collapse. Patience involves understanding that technical glitches and delays are natural things in the virtual world. So you will have to resist your inner Hulk whenever the screen of one of our team members freezes right in the middle of a meeting. For the dash of paprika, that is the secret weapon. Try to spice up video calls with funny backgrounds and quirky filters. No one can resist a leader who wears a different kind of hat in every meeting.

When it comes to virtual meetings, they can either be a curse or a blessing, based on how someone tries to use them. Never be the leader who keeps back-to-back meetings or video calls. In place of doing so, you will have to turn yourself into the hero who opts for focused and shorter meetings with precise agendas. In case someone from your team suggests having all the meetings at once for about two hours, remind them that even shows on Netflix come with intermissions.

But here is something that you need to understand. Effective communication is not only about conveying information in the right way. It also involves the creation of a sense of closeness, keeping aside the distance. It is about keeping in mind the members of your team are a lot more than simple faces on the screen. They are true human beings with true lives. So never hesitate to ask them about their pets, weekend plans, or the Netflix show they are binging. It is all about such little moments of connection that can make remote work feel a little less remote.

OVERCOMING CHALLENGES: EMPATHY TO THE RESCUE

Management of remote teams comes with its own set of challenges that need special solutions. Opting for hybrid teams that comprise both physically present employees in the workplace and remote employees can help organizations improve productivity, lower costs, and be more agile in the face of adversities. But managing remote teams is a lot different than managing employees in the workplace.

Here are some of the challenges of remote employee management and how you can deal with them as a leader.

Lack of Face-to-Face Supervision

As a leader, you might worry that the members of your remote team might not work as hard or efficiently as they would have in the physical workplace. On the other hand, your team members might struggle with less access to leadership communication and support. It can easily make remote employees feel that their leader is not in touch with their requirements and is not supportive of getting the work done. To deal with this, you will have to opt for daily or weekly check-ins. Creating project milestones with proper deadlines can help. Also, never forget to discuss potential obstacles and ongoing progress.

Remote Coaching

Remote coaching can turn out to be a true challenge. Face-to-face coaching always comes with the extra advantage of observing your team members and providing them feedback. In order to take care of this, start by scheduling remote coaching time. You can also opt for the five-step approach where you will *explain, demonstrate, make them try, track performance,* and *redirect* them. You will have to ensure that you are available all the time to answer all kinds of questions or clear doubts.

Keeping the Communication Flowing

It is one of the easiest things to do in the physical world to get to your team members and discuss ideas or have a brainstorming meeting for a new issue. Doing so provides everyone with the chance to speak freely. However, in remote work, the tendency is to opt for text messages and emails instead of opting for personal communication methods. It ends up increasing the chances of misunderstandings. In order to take care of this, try to organize one-on-one virtual meetings so that you can understand the difficulties faced by your team members or any of their concerns. Also, being transparent can help in a remote work setting where the goal is clear.

Work–Life Balance

It has been found that while remote work is a convenient option, it comes with certain downsides as well. The lack of a proper boundary between life and work is a great issue. With time, team members who cannot find a balance between work and life might face issues. You, as a leader, have to set a work schedule for the whole team and also try your best to stick to it, for instance, no work calls after 8 p.m. Another thing that can be done from your side is to respect the weekend time of your team members.

THE IMPACT OF EMPATHETIC REMOTE LEADERSHIP

Alright, my fellow leaders, let us now have a look at leadership in the age of working in sweatpants right from our couches. The sudden uprising of remote work has turned most of us into digital explorers, always navigating the terrain of Slack messages, video calls, and the battle with Wi-Fi signals. As already said earlier, empathy can help a lot when it comes to remote leadership. It is like your ticket to develop a connected, strong, and awesome team, regardless of where everyone is located. A survey found that about 64% of employees agree that remote work helped enhance their productivity (Frank

L., 2022). I don't think that would have been possible without an empathetic leader by their side. But are you aware of the impact of empathetic remote leadership?

To start with, you will have to ditch the old-school leadership book that suggests you need to be harsh to be an effective leader. You will have to act like the virtual guide of your remote team where you will lead your team with compassion and understanding. Instead of saying, "Why isn't the project complete yet?" try to ask, "What help can I do to finish the project in the right way?" It is more or less like replacing a rude office security guard with a cute and friendly office mascot. I hope you get the difference.

Speaking of support, you can never forget about the power of active listening. When a member of your team vents about their problematic Wi-Fi, stay away from the urge to share your own Wi-Fi stories. Try to nod to what they say in understanding. You can also throw in an empathetic, "I can feel your problem." It is like a therapy session where there is no couch and awkward silence. When you show support for your team members, you can easily develop loyalty and trust within the team (Runyon, 2021). Nothing can be better than this, right?

Now comes the real deal. Empathetic leadership is not only about being a great listener. You will also need to take action (Gupta & Gupta, 2022). For instance, when one of your team members is drowning in consequent deadlines, you can provide them with a virtual lifebuoy. You can offer them additional resources, offer to shuffle tasks, or even use your power as a leader to extend the deadlines when required. Always keep in mind that a bit of flexibility can go a long way in the realm of remote work.

Next comes team morale. It is more or less like the pot of gold right at the end of the rainbow. As an empathetic leader, it is your duty to sprinkle the pot of gold with recognition, words of encouragement, and occasional GIFs that can easily capture the collective mood of the whole team. You will have to understand that empathetic remote leadership is more like a ripple effect.

As you start leading a remote team with empathy, the members of your team can feel heard, seen, and valued. Their chances of being motivated, engaged, and willing to go the extra distance to finish a task will be quite high. Start using your superpowers to develop a remote work environment that is not only ready to provide you with results but is also filled with true human connections.

CHAPTER 6:
NAVIGATING THE STORM—EMPATHETIC LEADERSHIP AMID CRISIS

A leader takes people where they want to go. A great leader takes people where they don't necessarily want to go, but ought to be.
–Rosalynn Carter

Empathetic leadership—the shining knight in armor who is always there to rescue the team when the world is in commotion. Well, being an empathetic leader is not only about having an idea when to send out virtual pats on the back or a funny meme on regular working days. It is also about wearing your superhero cape and jumping in whenever your team comes across any kind of crisis, all set to save the day.

Try to think of this—your team is right in the middle of a big project, and the virtual office gets hit by a huge storm. No, I am not talking about thunderstorms, but a storm of technical issues that could easily give competition to any sci-fi movie. Everyone is sitting in front of a frozen screen, files have disappeared into the digital world, and the once "superhero" Wi-Fi has changed into a cat that is coming and going at its own will. It is right where empathetic leadership comes into play. In place of getting panicked and sending out emails in all caps (all of us have experienced this), an empathetic leader would calm themselves down and say, "Okay, we are in this together. Let us figure out what can be done." It is similar to being a calm captain of a ship right in the middle of a thunderstorm.

Do you know what is the real deal with empathetic leadership at the time of a crisis? It is not about trying to keep your cool. It is about truly caring for the well-being of your entire team. You will have to constantly check in with your team members, ask them how they are trying to hold up against the digital storm and provide support.

Then comes the power of humor. Situations of crisis might seem like a roller coaster that does not seem to end along with a side of turbulence. It is right when a funny meme or a superb joke can turn out to be a ray of sunshine through the clouds of a storm. A bit of humor can help relieve all the tension and remind the team that all of us are in the glitchy spaceship together.

Keep in mind that the most important aspect of an empathetic leader in the face of crisis is the ability to adapt and change direction. When a plan tends to fall apart, an empathetic leader would never try to cling to the ship with a hole. They would grab a lifeboat and steer the entire team in the direction of a new course while trying to keep the morale of the team high. Let us delve deeper into how empathetic leadership can help during a crisis.

THE ROLE OF EMPATHY IN CRISIS MANAGEMENT

Let me start this section with some real-world examples. During the 2008 financial crisis, the CEO of JPMorgan Chase, Jamie Dimon, empathetically communicated the bank's strategy and reassured employees about their job security (The Economic Times, 2023). Another one is when the COVID-19 pandemic hit, Satya Nadella, CEO of Microsoft, empathetically communicated with his global team, acknowledging the stress and uncertainty they were facing (Bhan, 2023). What can you understand from these examples? It is empathetic leadership that is required at the time of a crisis and that can make such big organizations stand up in the face of crisis.

Crisis management might feel like trying to juggle flaming bowling pins while being on a unicycle over a pit of crocodiles. It can never be regarded as a walk in the park. However, the moment you can sprinkle a bit of empathy into the whole mix, you can be the circus master and make the crocodiles do cha-cha. Empathy at the time of crisis management is about understanding that the members of your team are not like gears in a machine. They are real human beings who also have quirks, feelings, and occasional affairs with the office plant (do not judge; all of us have been here). So you can say,

"Hey, I am well aware that this situation is feeling like a roller coaster that does not seem to end. How can I support you all from my end?"

Communicating at the time of a crisis is similar to transmitting a message through a paper cup telephone while you are on a roller coaster. But empathetic leaders tend to make sure that the message is clear, just like an Instagram photo with the perfect filter. The real magic of empathy in crisis management is in the process of making decisions. A leader who uses empathy in the workplace would never sit in an ivory tower, making decisions that might affect the members of the team. An empathetic leader is someone who would gather the whole team around the table, request their input, and consider their perspectives all the time. It might feel like directing a hit movie and allowing the actors to have a say in the script. I hope you can get my point.

Next comes adaptability. Crisis management is like trying your best to solve a Rubik's cube while having your eyes closed—you would never get to know which way is up. Empathetic leaders would never stick to one solution as if it is the only lifeline. They are flexible by nature, and they can adapt to situations with multiple solutions in hand.

Handling Workplace Crisis as an Empathetic Leader

Try to picture this: Your workplace is similar to a pressure cooker with the heat cranked up. Deadlines are running behind you all faster than a hungry lion trying to chase a burger truck, and the client just dropped a new bomb of a project on the desk that is a lot bigger than your vacation suitcase. This is what the workplace crisis looks like, my fellow leaders. However, there is nothing to worry about, as empathy is there for you.

Let us define the hero. Empathy is not about making the best "I can feel your problem" face and giving sympathy pats on the back. If you think of it like that, you are wrong. Empathy is like the pass to the wide array of emotions that the team members are dealing with. It involves stepping into their shoes and saying, "I have been here."

Do you want to use empathy to deal with workplace crises? Here's how empathy can help:

- *The power of understanding*: At the time of a crisis, tensions are bound to run higher than the necktie of a giraffe. However, an empathetic leader would never fan the flames. They would drench the fire with some sprinkles of understanding. So when a member of your team tends to fume as the project deadline has been moved up, in place of saying, "Just calm down. It does not look that bad," say, "I can completely understand your frustration. Why don't we try to figure this out together?"

- *Crystal clear communication*: Communication is the key at the time of a crisis. However, the truth is that it might be tangled just like a bunch of headphones in your bag. An empathetic leader will always try to be clear with what they say. As you send out emails related to a crisis, do not try to hide the necessary stuff under corporate speak. Try your best to keep things straightforward. Additionally, you can add a witty subject line and lighten the mood.

- *Collaborative approach over chaos*: When faced with a crisis, it is quite easy to get yourself into lone wolf mode as a leader, trying to solve everything alone. However, an empathetic leader will always opt for collaboration. Offer assistance, reach out to your team members, and ask for their input. After all, who would not like to be a superhero who is surrounded by other caped team members?

- *Using the power of flexibility*: You might not have any idea which way to turn at the time of a crisis. Empathy can provide you with the power of adaptability. So be open to new solutions, change direction when required, and be flexible, similar to a yoga teacher. When you have empathy by your side, you will not only be surviving the crisis, but you will also be conquering it while putting a smile on everyone's face.

BALANCING BUSINESS NEEDS AND EMPATHY DURING CRISIS

Trying to balance business needs and the emotional well-being of your team members is a tricky thing to do. It is tricky, but nothing is impossible. The needs of a business are like huge and hungry monsters that demand to be fed all the time.

Quarterly reports, deadlines, and targets—all of them roaring for attention. But here is the thing: Empathetic leadership is not about allowing the business beast to run around wild. It is all about trying to tame it using a velvet glove. Let me make this simpler for you: It involves understanding that a business has got appetites, the members of your team have also got feelings. How can someone juggle both?

Think of this: You are in an important meeting with a client, trying to discuss the next big project that requires to be completed within two days. You might try to respond with a frantic, "No worries, everything will be done ASAP." Or you might try to channel the inner diplomat and say something like, "We are on it. But let us discuss how this can be turned into reality without trying to set the office on fire." Can you see the difference?

You can never forget the well-being of your employees. They are breathing humans with emotions. When they get overwhelmed, stressed, or cannot deal with the Monday workload, it is an empathetic leader who notices. So here is the plan of action—you come across a member of your team who looks like they have just survived a thunderstorm. In place of trying to pretend that everything is okay, unleash your empathetic side and say, "I just noticed that you are not your usual fighting self. Would you like to talk about something?"

At a time of crisis, you can never forget about setting realistic expectations. It is like telling your friend that you will get ready in five minutes when you are in your pajamas. Empathetic leaders would never overpromise and underdeliver. They try to be transparent regarding all that is feasible. As you try to communicate the situation with your team members with honesty, they will not feel like they are repeatedly dealing with broken promises.

In my tenure as the CEO of Steel City Pops, we navigated a multitude of challenges, especially during the time of the COVID-19 pandemic. Our business, already in a transitional phase after a Chapter 11 restructuring, was put to the ultimate test by the crisis. During this hard time, empathetic leadership became not just a managerial strategy but a necessity. Firstly, acknowledging the emotions of our employees was crucial. They were going through their own difficulties, worrying not just about their jobs but also about their health and well-being and that of their families. Our weekly meetings became safe spaces for candid conversations where everyone felt heard and empowered to express their ideas and concerns. I was intentional in asking for feedback and taking the time to listen. As a leader, I had to set the example that it was okay to acknowledge our vulnerabilities. I also understood that emotional intelligence was needed as much as business acumen.

During the initial days of the stay-at-home orders, sales were almost nonexistent. While we scrambled to pivot our business model, I wore a bracelet with a message that read, "Smooth Seas Never Made a Skilled Sailor." It was a physical token to remind not just myself but also my team that we had to navigate through this crisis, no matter how stormy the seas. We tapped into our collective creativity to find new revenue streams, such as partnering with local HOA groups and neighborhoods to bring pops directly to communities. It was an innovation born out of necessity but also deeply rooted in empathy for what our customers were going through. We knew people were stuck at home, and we wanted to bring a little joy to their doorsteps. We also developed new products, ranging from pop floats to gourmet popcorn, while setting up a national shipping program to bring our offerings to a larger audience.

We faced setbacks, like the second wave of COVID affecting our sales more than usual, but it was empathetic leadership that held us together. When you make decisions with empathy, you're not just concerned with the bottom line; you care about the impact of those decisions on your team and your customers. The mantra of giving talented people the freedom to make decisions, asking for and acting on feedback, and not chasing after every seemingly profitable idea but staying true to our core values helped us stay resilient. While I am proud of how we pivoted and innovated during this crisis, I am most thankful for the sense of community and mutual respect we built among our team. Empathetic leadership helped us navigate the crisis by making every challenge a shared experience and every triumph a collective victory.

PRACTICAL STRATEGIES FOR LEADING WITH EMPATHY IN CRISIS

A crisis can turn out to be a hard time for any kind of organization, whether it is a scandal, a pandemic, or a natural disaster. The way in which you communicate with the stakeholders can end up making a huge difference in the way you deal with the situation. Here are some of the ways in which you can communicate using empathy and compassion at the time of a crisis.

Understand the Audience

The very first step in communicating with empathy at the time of a crisis is to have an idea about the audience and also their emotions, expectations, and requirements. Different stakeholders might have different questions and needs based on the way the crisis impacts them. The members of your team might want to know how the crisis will impact their job security, safety, and arrangements of work, for instance. The partners of the organization might want to know about the impact of the crisis on the collaborations and contracts. In order to properly get an idea of your audience, use feedback forms, surveys, or direct channels of communication.

Be Honest

You will have to be honest and clear regarding the situation and the actions you take. Stay away from denying, exaggerating, or hiding the actual facts. Not being able to do so might end up impacting your trust and credibility. It is always better to acknowledge the hardships and reality and share clearly everything you know and all that you have no idea about. You will have to explain in clear words what you are trying to do to take care of the crisis. What you expect from your stakeholders should also be communicated in a clear and concise way. Keep providing timely and correct information while updating everyone when the situation changes. Stay away from jargon and technical terms and opt for concise and clear language.

Listen Properly and Respond

Listening is all about focusing on what others have to say and the way they say it. It also involves taking into account their feelings and views. Responding is all about answering the questions asked, addressing concerns, and trying to take care of the issues. If you want to listen and respond in the right way, try to use skills of active listening, like reflecting, paraphrasing, and summarizing. Open-ended questions can work like magic, such as, "What can be done from my side?" or, "How do you feel now?" to encourage engagement and dialogue.

Show Compassion and Empathy

You already know that empathy is about putting yourself in the shoes of others and trying to have an idea about their perspective. Compassion is all about offering support and showing care for their overall well-being. In order to show compassion and empathy, use phrases and words that can express your appreciation and concern. For instance, you can say, "I completely understand how tough the situation is for all of you," or, "We are in this together as a team." Sharing examples and stories of how others are dealing with the crisis can help.

Be Reliable and Consistent

It is necessary to be reliable and consistent in your communication. Reliability is about trying to fulfill all your commitments and promises, followed by checking in with what you communicate. Consistency indicates trying to deliver the same message across various platforms and channels while aligning your actions and words. You can opt for a plan of communication that would help in outlining all your channels, strategies, goals, and tone.

Be Hopeful

Being hopeful and positive are the characteristics of an empathetic leader. Positive means being able to highlight the achievements and strengths of the organization and recognizing the contributions and hard work of your team members. You will have to express optimism, resilience, and confidence while dealing with the crisis and inspire everyone in your team to do the same. Opt for phrases and words that can help in conveying encouragement and praise. For instance, saying, "I am truly grateful for the kind of support I have received from you all," or, "I am sure we can deal with this challenge as a team" can help.

POST-CRISIS: USING EMPATHY TO REBUILD AND HEAL

Try to think of this: Your organization just survived a huge crisis that was similar to a soap opera with numerous plot twists. Now the time has come that you pick up all the pieces, and you will require empathy for this. Let's have a look at how empathy can be used to lead your team to the land of healing and recovery.

- *Taking into account the emotional wounds*: After a period of crisis, emotions are bound to run high. As an empathetic leader, you will have to stay away from sweeping all such emotions under the rug. In place of doing so, you will have to try and acknowledge them. You can say, "Hello, team. I am well aware that it was tough. Let us discuss it." It is more or less like shining a torchlight on the emotional baggage that every member of your team has been carrying around.

- *Acknowledging the issue*: You will need to acknowledge the issue and also take responsibility for it. Never try to hide things or blame other people for what has happened. Try your best to be transparent and honest regarding the impact and facts. Share the actions that you will take to put things back on track.

- *Assessing the damage*: The next important thing that you will need to do is assess the damage and try to find out the cause of the crisis. You will need to do an objective and detailed analysis of all those things that went wrong, the way it happened, and who was involved. It is your duty to decipher the weaknesses, failures, and gaps in your organization.

- *Rebuilding trust*: Right after a period of crisis, trust is something that might be more shattered than a dropped phone screen. It is your job to build it once again, placing one brick at a time. Be transparent and honest, and show others that everything you do will be committed to a better future.

- *Learning and improving*: After the crisis period is over, it is necessary to reflect and learn from the overall experience. What exactly went wrong? What are the things that can be done differently? An empathetic leader would always try to opt for open discussion regarding the things that can be improved without taking part in the blame game.

In the end, being an empathetic leader to heal and rebuild after a crisis is like being the captain of a huge ship that is going through stormy waters. You will have to mend the sails, guide the entire team through the turbulence, and make sure that everyone on board feels heard and understood.

CHAPTER 7:
NAVIGATING DIFFICULT WATERS—EMPATHY IN TOUGH CONVERSATIONS

The mediocre teacher tells. The good teacher explains. The superior teacher demonstrates. The great teacher inspires.
–William Arthur Ward

Tough conversations are quite common in the corporate sector. Yes, you guessed it right. I am talking about all those sweat-inducing and heart-pounding dialogues that can make you feel like going back to elementary school and trading Pokémon cards instead. But all of us are grown-ups now, and it will not be the right thing to try and escape the sticky situations where you will need to channel the inner negotiator, diplomat, and at times, the stand-up comedian.

The aim of this section is to make you understand the art of using empathy in tough conversations. Let us try to be honest here: Such conversations cannot be regarded as a barrel of laughs. They are mostly like a ride on a roller coaster without any safety harness, filled with turns, twists, and all those moments when you feel like you need to have another cup of coffee. However, there is nothing to be scared of as I will share various ways in which you can unleash the power of empathy to sail through the stormy waters like a pro.

THE ART OF EMPATHETIC FEEDBACK

Let us talk about something that is quite rare in the office culture—empathetic feedback. Yes, I am talking about that magical approach to providing feedback that will not leave your team members diving under their desks or running for the hills. Try to think of this—you are ready to provide feedback to your team member, Jonathan. Now Jonathan is someone who is more or less like a wizard with spreadsheets. However, when it comes to punctuality, he turns into a wizard with a not-so-reliable wand. How are you going to approach this kind of situation with empathy?

Empathetic feedback is about trying to speak the language of emotional understanding. It is all about trying to understand that Jonathan has his own perspective, his own set of reasons to be late all the time, and his own affair with the snooze button every morning.

Importance of Empathetic Feedback

Here are some of the reasons why empathetic feedback is so important in the workplace:

- *The trust factor*: Think of yourself in a room with some people you barely know. Suddenly, they start to throw tomatoes at you. It cannot be regarded as a pleasant picture, right? That is what feedback would feel like without empathy. As you try to provide feedback with empathy, you can start building trust. Your entire team will know that you are not here to attack them with criticism. You truly want all of them to grow. It is like being the friendly sugar supplier in the neighborhood.

- *Boosts morale*: When there is no empathy, feedback might hamper morale and deflate the same much faster than a popped balloon. However, when you try to add empathy to the mix, you will be adding helium to the balloon. You will be able to lift up your team members, motivate them to keep working hard for excellence, and make them feel valued.

- *The game of improvement*: Feedback is not at all about picking out flaws and leaving it just like that. It is all about helping the members of your team to be the best version of themselves. You can think of empathetic feedback as a road map in the direction of improvement. You will not only be saying, "You failed to reach the mark," but you will say, "You might have missed the mark, but here is how it is possible to hit the bullseye the next time you try."

- *Conflict resolution*: Have you ever been in a heated argument and had a person listen to what you said without any kind of judgment? It might feel like adding water to a firepit where things will suddenly start to cool down. Empathetic feedback comes with the power to defuse conflicts simply by making others feel heard and understood.

- *The learning loop*: Empathetic feedback is about changing the feedback loop into a magical loop of learning. You provide feedback, the members of your team grow, and the entire process will keep repeating. It is more like a cycle of improvement that can help everyone to keep moving ahead in the direction of success.

Empathetic feedback is a lot more than a buzzword. It is the secret of effective leadership. It can help in the development of trust, boost morale, aid improvement, and take care of conflicts.

How to Navigate Difficult Conversations

Everyone might try to get emotional, defensive, or argumentative when they feel they are judged or accused. However, when tough conversations are taken care of with kindness, anyone can get to reflect on the issue. The problem is not with the words that are used but the way in which they are delivered. Feedback is a necessary tool for the improvement of skills, relationships, and performances. However, it might also turn out to be a challenge to give. If you tend to lack empathy, you might get portrayed as insensitive, harsh, or defensive.

Here are some of the ways in which you can navigate difficult conversations with the help of empathy.

- *Clear communication*: Tough conversations tend to arise whenever there is a requirement to provide constructive feedback, address issues, or discuss challenging things with the members of your team. But an empathetic leader can always understand that clarity is necessary. By conveying the message in a clear way, a leader can make sure that the team members can understand the situation they are dealing with and can work together in the direction of resolution or improvement. Effective communication is powerful enough to develop a pathway for development and growth, allowing everyone to learn from their mistakes and attain their full potential.

- *Firmness coupled with respect*: Difficult conversations come with the requirement of a specific level of firmness, as leaders are required to address issues or deliver corrective measures. But it is important to maintain an empathetic and respectful approach at the time of conversations. Genuine leaders can always understand that respect is something that can foster collaboration and trust in a team. As you start to treat the members of your team with dignity, you will be able to develop an environment that promotes open dialogue and makes sure that everyone feels heard and valued.

- *Emotional intelligence*: Emotional intelligence is often regarded as an important trait for leaders, especially at the time of dealing with tough conversations. It involves understanding and recognizing emotions in others and also in yourself and utilizing the understanding to direct interactions in the right way. Skilled leaders always try to tap into their emotional intelligence to stay composed, calm, and empathetic at times of hard conversations. They listen actively, validate problems or concerns, and try to understand varying perspectives, developing a setting of mutual understanding and respect.

- *Reflect instead of react*: In difficult conversations, take your time not to jump to conclusions or turn on your defensive mode. Try your best to put yourself in the shoes of the other person. Understand how much courage it might have taken for the person to share their concerns and focus on their opinion and perspective.

NAVIGATING CONFLICT WITH EMPATHY

Most of us tend to get along with the people we work with. However, at the time of conflict, no one seems to be concerned about what most people are actually doing. All they are concerned about is the all-caps fight that breaks out on email chains. Conflicts keep taking place, even among professionals who are mature enough. It has been found that employees in today's world tend to spend about 2.8 hours every week dealing with conflicts at the workplace. In fact, for about 29% of employees, conflict at the workplace seems to be constant (Pollack Peacebuilding Systems, n.d.).

Getting to Know the Nature of Conflict

Right before you can dive into strategies for resolving conflicts, it is important that you have a clear understanding of the conflict nature. It is possible that conflict might arise from multiple sources and might end up having both negative and positive impacts on an organization. As you get to recognize the various aspects of conflict, you can equip yourself in a better way to manage conflicts.

Conflicts might take up various forms, right from normal disagreements to full-fledged arguments. The primary cause behind it could be anything like differences in beliefs, values, or opinions. Or it might be due to external factors like changes in organizational priorities or changes in the market. Generally, conflict is categorized into four types.

- *Process conflicts*: It arises from differences regarding how to proceed with an initiative or project. One of the classic process conflicts is "You are completely doing it wrong." Such conflicts are mild by nature, specifically when the members of your team agree on the task goals.
- *Status conflicts*: It is when people argue regarding who is in charge. It is quite common in workplaces and is generally the result of a power clash.

- *Task conflicts*: Such conflicts are about the goals of a project or the primary reason why someone is doing a task in the first place. Due to the fundamental misalignment, such conflicts are harder than process conflicts.

- *Relationship conflicts*: Conflicts of this kind can turn out to be trickier as they tend to generate when feelings end up getting personal. Such conflicts might develop feelings of bullying, disrespect, or being unwelcome on a team.

How Conflict Affects Organizations and Teams

As already said earlier, conflicts can have both negative and positive consequences based on the way it gets managed. When taken care of in the right way, conflict can help spark creativity, help in personal growth, and enhance problem-solving by focusing on various kinds of perspectives. For instance, when your team finds it hard to come up with ideas for a new campaign, a healthy debate regarding various approaches can help in attaining a more effective solution. However, when conflicts are managed poorly or when they are left unresolved, it might lead to reduced morale, decreased productivity, and bad connections among the members of your team.

Unresolved conflicts are well-known for the development of a toxic work environment. As a leader, it is necessary to understand the importance of focusing on conflicts early on and making sure that all kinds of disagreements are taken care of in a positive way. It involves encouraging active listening, fostering open communication and developing a culture of empathy within the team.

Conflict Resolution and the Role of a Leader

Leaders play an important role in resolving conflicts by setting up the tone for a proper work environment and leading by example. Here are some of the ways in which a leader can help in conflict resolution:

- *Setting the tone of the work environment*: It is your duty as a leader to create a work environment where trust, open communication, and respect are on the priority list. It all starts with the behavior of the leader, as they need to demonstrate an attitude of open-mindedness and collaboration. For instance, a leader can promote a proper working environment by organizing activities that can help in building teams or where the members can get to know one another in a better way.

- *Promoting feedback and open communication*: One of the key aspects of conflict resolution is to foster a setting where feedback and open communication are encouraged. As a leader creates a safe environment for the team members where they can share their concerns and thoughts, misunderstandings can be prevented quite easily. You can encourage open communication by

having one-on-one meetings with every member to
learn about their goals and concerns.

- *Leading by example*: For the effective management of
conflicts within the team, it is important to lead by
example. Simply by modeling conflict resolution
behaviors and skills, you can always encourage the
team members to look at disagreements in a solution-
oriented and constructive way.

Conflict Resolution Strategies

You will have to understand that conflict is a natural part
of any kind of team dynamics. I know it is challenging and
uncomfortable to deal with, but it is also a chance to develop
and grow. Here are some of the ways in which you can take
care of conflicts in the workplace:

- *Empathy and active listening*: No matter how many times
I have mentioned these in this book, it is never enough
when it comes to empathy and active listening. During
the early days of my career, I acted dishonestly in a
situation. Aimee, my district manager, handled the
situation in a way that was both constructive and firm.
You might not believe this, but she took me out to
lunch to talk about the issue and made me understand
that my career would be hampered if I continued
on this path. What can you learn from this? It was
Aimee's ability to confront such a hard issue in a way
that provided me with room for self-improvement and

growth. She could have easily acted out or could have refused to even listen to my part. But she chose the softer way—she used active listening and empathy. You will have to listen first before judging a situation or a person.

- *Determining the root cause*: The moment conflicts arise, it is necessary to take the time so that you can dig deeper and get to know the underlying problems that are at play. This would need asking questions and opting for open communication among the people who are involved. For example, if two members of your team are in conflict because of a project deadline, it would be helpful to find out why each of them is feeling pressured to meet the deadline. It could be the case that one of them is worried about the client, while the other might be concerned about the work quality.

- *Finding common ground*: As you determine the root cause, it is now time to work in the direction of resolution. You will have to brainstorm proper solutions while focusing on the interests of all the parties and being open to finding common ground. Suppose two members of your team are in conflict over how they can approach a new client. By asking them to work together and share the ideas they have got, you might get to understand that both of them have great insights.

LEADING DIFFICULT CONVERSATIONS: LAYOFFS AND PERFORMANCE ISSUES

Now we are ready to deal with the "L" word—layoffs. Do you know who is the cranky cousin of layoffs? It is a performance issue. Both involve tough conversations that most leaders are not aware of how to deal with. Such conversations need more finesse than solving a Rubik's cube with your eyes closed.

Let us start with layoffs. Layoffs are no less than delivering a surprise party invitation; however, in place of a cake, it comes with a pink slip inside. You can never regard layoffs to be a joyous thing. But you can always try and take care of them with empathy.

- *Being honest and gentle*: Honesty is more or like broccoli; you might like it, but it is not everyone's favorite. As you try to deliver the news of layoffs, it is best to be direct yet gentle. There is no need to sugarcoat things. However, make sure that you do not end up blurting it out like reading a weather forecast. Give your best to use empathy so that you can acknowledge the impact that the layoffs have on your team. You can say something like, "I know that this is not easy news to accept."

- *Acknowledging feelings*: The members of your team might react differently to layoffs, experiencing various emotions that would range from sadness to anger to confusion. It is more or less like trying to guess the flavor of jelly beans in a room with no lights—you can never be sure what you will get. You will have to acknowledge all such feelings in an empathetic way. Say something like, "I can completely understand that it is hard, and what you are feeling is completely valid."

- *Providing support*: Layoffs can feel like a curveball in a game of catch. The members of your team didn't see it coming. It is quite evident that the news will throw them off balance. You will have to showcase empathy by providing support. You can help them search for new jobs, provide recommendations, or simply be a listening ear. You will have to be the friend who brings ice cream (or maybe a beer, just kidding) after a breakup.

- *Communicating the why*: Layoffs are like a riddle without any proper answer. You will have to help the team members understand the actual reasons behind the layoffs. Try your best to be transparent. It would be something like, "Here's why we had to end up making this decision."

Now let us focus on performance issues. Such conversations might be as pleasant as trying to deal with a herd of cats, but they are important for improvement and growth. Here's how you can communicate with empathy regarding performance issues.

- *Get started with the positives*: Similar to offering a carrot before you offer a broccoli, you will have to start with the positives. Try to throw light on the achievements and strengths of the team members. It involves saying things like, "You have seriously done some superb work on all these projects."

- *Active listening*: As you try to discuss performance issues, it is important that you listen to the other person actively. Simply nodding and smiling will not work. You will have to ask questions so that you get to understand the perspective of the employee. It is more or less like a detective who is trying to solve a great mystery: "Why don't you share some of the challenges that you faced while trying to meet deadlines?"

- *Being specific*: Dealing with performance issues might feel like trying to hit the bullseye in the dark. You will need to use empathy by being specific regarding the concerns and issues. You can say, "In recent days, I have noticed a sudden decline in your project submission rates."

- *Providing support*: Plans for improving performance are similar to gym memberships—they can be more effective when you try and use them. So try to provide support, training, or resources to help the team member improve. You can be the personal trainer for their corporate growth.

You will have to make sure that you address particular actions or behaviors and do not make any kind of judgment regarding the character of your team member. As you discuss performance issues, using "I" statements can help in expressing what you have observed. For instance, you can say, "I have noticed a sudden decline in your project completion rate. Would you like to share what is bothering you?" Trying to deal with performance issues in an empathetic way would need a combination of clear communication, understanding, and a commitment to help the related team member succeed. By using empathy to approach such situations, you will not only be able to address the issues at hand but also get to foster a culture of support and trust within the team.

Tough conversations related to performance issues and layoffs can never be an easy thing to deal with. However, with the help of a bit of empathy, you can make such conversations more productive and manageable. Always keep in mind that empathy is like a magic wand that can easily change an uncomfortable conversation into a new chance for growth and understanding.

CHAPTER 8:
EMPATHY—THE GAME CHANGER IN LEADERSHIP

If your actions create a legacy that inspires others to dream more, learn more, do more and become more, then, you are an excellent leader.
–Dolly Parton

Picture this—you walk into the office with a confident demeanor, all set to deal with the day's challenges. But there is a twist! In place of trying to bark out orders like an honorable commander in boots, you channel your inner Yoda—patient, wise, and incredibly empathetic. Empathetic leadership is not only about being able to understand the feelings of your team members. It also involves sprinkling some productivity-boosting fairy dust on the team. As you take your time to get to know the fears, hopes, and dreams of your entire team, there is something magical that takes place. Do you know what it is? The members of your team feel seen, valued, and appreciated.

Think of your team meetings turning into hubs of brainstorming excellence. When you opt for empathetic leadership, the voice of everyone will be heard, right from the extroverted idea tornadoes to the introverted inventors. You will get to create a safe space where ideas can flow freely, just like a chocolate fountain at a lavish party.

THE EMPATHY EFFECT: A LOOK AT TEAM DYNAMICS

Empathy and the ability to connect with others are important skills in our professional as well as personal lives. In the workplace, empathy tends to be an important component for emotional competence and efficient leadership. In fact, as we already know, it can help in the improvement of human connections. Empathy is important in the workplace for any kind of organization that is dealing with underperformance, setbacks, or people who really want to attain something. But why do leaders find it hard to be empathetic at work? The primary reason behind this is empathy needs effort, patience, and time to develop. It is not something that you can develop in a day. Want to know how empathy can impact the dynamics of your team?

Enhanced Communication

You can think of empathy as the universal workplace translator. It can provide you all the help to tune into each of your team members' wavelengths, understand the vibe they carry, and then respond in accordance to that. When you can successfully empathize with your team members and listen to them actively, communication can become as smooth as a buttered slide.

Try to think of this: In place of crossed wires and misunderstandings, every member of your team is tossing ideas back and forth, just like a tennis match, and nodding in agreement. All of them are on the same page, and there is no requirement for interpretive dance moves to convey the idea or point (you can surely do so if that's the thing of your team).

Better Team Bonding

Empathy can act like a bonding glue that can help in holding a complete team together. When you take out the necessary time to understand the points of your team members on a personal level, you end up creating a sense of unity that is a lot stronger than you can actually imagine. Suddenly, the whole team would feel like one family, putting aside the awkward family holiday dinners. You will surely find yourself sharing hobbies, cracking jokes, and maybe even tackling escape rooms as a team. In the end, the office will no longer be a place to work. It will turn into a large community where everyone has got each other's back.

Improved Morale

I am sure you can remember all those days when the energy level of your whole team felt like a punctured flat tire. Empathy can help in pumping up the flat tire of team morale. When a leader truly cares for the well-being of every team member and gets to know what exactly can make them tick, such a leader can turn into a superhero who has the power to boost morale. You might not be aware of this, but a simple, "Hey, guys, how's everything going?" can make a world of difference. Every member of your team will start feeling as if they are soaring on a cloud of support and appreciation. There will be no more dragging feet. Everyone will bounce into the office on a daily basis with the same kind of enthusiasm that a kid has while entering a toy shop.

Resolution of Conflicts

Let's be honest here—conflicts in the workplace are as avoidable as bad hair days. However, it is right where empathy can get into the picture, like a superhero who knows how to maintain peace. As you get to understand the emotions and perspectives behind every kind of conflict, you can equip yourself with a better way to get to a solution that would satisfy everyone on the team. There will be no more passive-aggressive email threads or Post-it notes. The best thing about empathy is that it can change conflicts into new chances of compromise and growth. You can become the mediator that everyone on your team will turn to whenever they require conflict resolution. You can be the peacekeeper.

Enhanced Productivity

Most leaders are not aware of this, but empathy could be used as a productivity hack that can work without an app. When your team knows that their leader truly cares about their concerns and well-being, they will get more motivated to try and give their best efforts. They will no longer be punching the clock and will be more invested in taking the team toward success. Every task will be taken care of with enthusiasm, and deadlines will get less daunting.

Improved Creativity

Apart from all the other benefits of empathy in the workplace, it can be used as a tool that can help in boosting creativity. When the members of your team don't think twice before expressing their ideas or thoughts, despite how wild they may be, creativity will thrive. Empathetic leaders come with the power to develop a work environment where brainstorming sessions would feel like explosions of new innovations. With a bit of empathy in the mix, your team will never be scared of suggesting an unconventional resolution or presenting an offbeat idea. You can never be sure whether a huge breakthrough might be waiting for the organization right behind a quirky idea.

Empathy can play a harmonious tune in the symphony of team dynamics that can help in bringing each and every instrument in a sweet unison. It is a lot more than a soft skill. It is something that can change your entire team into a high-performing machine. If you are a leader who is willing to inspire the team or looking out for ideas to do so, keep in mind that you have always got the superpower of empathy. Opt for it, use it, and watch the dynamics of your team change into something extraordinary. After all, teamwork can make the dream work, and empathy can always make it a dream that is worth running after.

PRODUCTIVITY AND EMPATHY: MORE THAN JUST NUMBERS

Any kind of business that comes with the goal of succeeding will surely be aware of the importance of productivity. However, here's the thing—workplace productivity depends to a great extent on the person who leads the herd. A team leader is required to have the necessary set of values and qualities that can encourage, motivate, and guide the employees. It is true that every leadership value tends to affect a team in their respective ways. But there is one value that always stays above the rest. Yes, you guessed it right. I am talking about empathy here. One of the most common ways in which empathy can help in boosting productivity is by keeping the members of your team in check. The majority of employees look to their team leader for appreciation and validation. In case they do not get their dues, it can result in a decline in team morale, besides giving rise to workplace unhappiness. I am sure it is something that you would never wish for.

Do you want to know more about how empathy can help in boosting productivity? Let me share them with you.

Empathy Can Boost Employee Engagement

Try to think of this—you are working on an important project, and your senior not only appreciates what you are doing but also wants to know how you are doing and listens to what you say in a genuine way. How would you feel? That is the power of empathy. When a leader shows empathy, everyone in the team will feel valued. Here's a quick thing for you: Engaged employees have higher chances of going the extra mile, dedicating the extra effort to exceed expectations and meet deadlines.

Improvement of Decision-Making

Empathy is not only a warm and fuzzy thing. It can also act as an important decision-making tool. As you try to put yourself in the shoes of others, you are most likely to come across perspectives and insights that you might not have been aware of before. It might feel like having a board of advisors right in your mind, a group that is always there to help you in making better decisions. Additionally, when your team knows that you will always make decisions while keeping their best interests in mind, they will always trust and support you no matter what decision you make.

Empathy and Collaboration

I have already said that teamwork can make the dream work. Empathy is something that can make collaboration feel like a breeze. When you get to understand the feelings and perspectives of your employees, you can easily work together in a better way. It is like getting a mental GPS that can guide you through every turn and twist as you plan a project. There will be less friction in the team when everyone feels respected and heard. As a result, you will get to channel more brainpower into solving problems.

Reduction of Stress

Let us now focus on the favorite topic of everyone in the workplace: stress. Do you know that empathy is well-known for reducing stress? When the members of your team know that you are someone who tries to understand the challenges they are facing and you are always there to support them, it can help release a lot of pressure from the pressure cooker. There is no need to say that when the levels of stress go down, levels of productivity will surely go up. It might feel like providing your team members with a mental spa day so that they can get back to work with a fresh mind and all set to conquer the tasks at hand.

Giving and Receiving Feedback Gets Easier

One of the most important elements of productivity is giving and receiving feedback. It is because feedback can provide us with a chance to improve. Empathy can permit leaders to get a proper understanding of why some areas are not up to the mark. Opting for an empathetic and compassionate approach to feedback will provide the members of your team with the necessary space to be open about the gaps and downfalls.

EMPATHY AND BUSINESS SUCCESS: A SYMBIOTIC RELATIONSHIP

In the fast-paced world of profits and losses, empathy is like the rocket fuel that can help in propelling business to new heights. Before we can jump into the nitty-gritty, let us first get on the same page regarding what empathy is in the context of business. Empathy means putting yourself in the shoes of your clients and employees and trying to understand their requirements. It also involves caring about their experiences. I am sure you might be thinking at this moment, "Isn't business all about strategies and profits?" Of course, it is. But there is a twist. Empathy can act as a profit enhancer. Let us find out how empathy can help in fueling the success of your business.

Better Customer Service

Have you ever heard of the phrase "actions speak louder than words"? It is quite true in the world of customer service. Empathetic leaders not only preach empathy; they try to live it. They tend to set the bar high by showcasing empathy in all their interactions with both their team members and customers.

Suppose you, the store manager in a retail store, are understanding, patient, and interested in solving the problem of customers. It can help set a tone that will echo in the team. With time, every member of your team will follow the same approach, developing an empathetic culture that customers can't help but notice.

When it comes to customer service, you can never forget trust. It acts as the bedrock of excellent customer service. When customers can feel valued and understood, their chances of trusting the company will increase. Empathetic leaders are well-known for creating a sense of trust simply by showcasing that they care about the emotions and concerns of the customers.

Try to think of an airline company with an empathetic CEO who takes the necessary time to personally respond to the feedback and complaints of customers. Besides being good PR, it is a demonstration of commitment to satisfying customers. As a result, customers will be more likely to go for that airline as they are sure that the company will go the extra mile to take care of their needs.

Assured Business Success

Effective communication can be regarded as the lifeblood of any business that is successful. Empathy can be the secret wand that helps translate the nuances of how we interact. Empathetic leaders can pick up on subtle cues, listen actively, and promote open dialogue.

Picture this: You are in a team meeting, and your senior, an empathetic leader, seeks your input and tries to consider all your ideas. It will no longer be a meeting, my fellow leaders. It will turn into a brainstorming bonanza. Do you know what the result will be? Streamlined workflows, innovative solutions, and a work environment where ideas can flow freely. All of these will lead to nothing but a successful business model.

High turnover rates are well-known for draining the morale and resources of a business. Empathetic leadership can turn out to be your secret weapon with which you can reduce turnover. When a leader can genuinely support and understand the team members, employees are more likely to stay. Think of a workplace where the overall management can recognize the unique needs of employees and provide opportunities for growth coupled with flexibility. It will act like a loyalty magnet. In a workplace of this kind, employees will not only stay but will also seek ways in which they can dedicate themselves to the success of the company.

Empathy Enhances Brand Reputation

When a brand shows empathy, it will act like a welcoming hug to all the customers. Whether it is trying to understand the pain points of customers or simply being there when they require support, empathy can help in forging a deep link that readily goes beyond monetary transactions.

Think of a company that listens actively to the feedback of customers, takes into account their concerns, and also takes necessary steps to take care of the issues. That is a brand that truly values empathy. Empathetic brands can also stand out in times of crisis. When the path gets tough, they don't provide empty platitudes. Such brands step up and take action. It can help in developing trust besides reinforcing their reputation as a brand that actually cares.

In today's world, where consumers get spoiled for choice, empathy can turn out to be the game changer. It is something that can change a brand from a business into a trusted partner in the lives of customers. Empathy can be the golden ticket to improving the reputation of your brand and also earning extended loyalty.

CHAPTER 9:
EMBRACING THE FUTURE—CULTIVATING EMPATHY IN LEADERSHIP

A leader is best when people barely know he exists, when his work is done, his aim fulfilled, they will say: we did it ourselves. —Lao Tzu

As work environments evolve faster than before in today's world, there exists one skill that is poised to be the defining trait of any successful leader. It is empathy. It could be a game changer in the coming time. Right before we can delve into empathy and its wonders, let us take a moment to truly appreciate the evolving work landscape of today. The traditional kind of office that we used to know is undergoing a huge transformation. Virtual collaboration, remote work, and fast changes have turned out to be the new normal. In such a dynamic work world, leadership would need a new set of qualities and skills.

THE GROWING IMPORTANCE OF EMPATHY IN LEADERSHIP

The work environments of today's world will keep shifting and diversifying. Due to this, the ability to connect, understand, and support every member of the team is more important than ever. You can say empathy has taken center stage in today's work environment. In the fast-paced world we live in today, uncertainty can be regarded as the only certainty. Do you know who can thrive in such environments? It is the empathetic leaders. They are the people who can clearly understand that change can turn out to be unsettling, and their team members might be dealing with uncertainty, too. With the help of empathy, they provide clarity, reassurance, and a steady hand on the wheel of the ship.

Try to think that you belong to a team that is led by a leader who is empathetic by nature. When the team gets hit by the winds of uncertainty, the person leading the team will not only give orders. They will also check in with every employee and address their fears and concerns. Such a kind of leadership can't only deal with storms but can also steer the entire ship through the strong winds with full confidence.

Adaptability is a new game in today's work culture. Teams are required to innovate, pivot, and stay agile. An empathetic leader can excel really well in fostering adaptability as they can very easily identify that every member of their team brings unique experiences, skills, and perspectives to the office table. Think of a leader who seeks input from every team member, regardless of their location or role in the company.

Such a leader understands that thought diversity can be a powerful asset. What is the result of this? A team that is not only adaptable but innovative as well.

Next comes resilience. It is the ability to bounce back from setbacks. You can think of this as a quality that is highly in demand. An empathetic leader will not only develop a team that is resilient but will also nurture resilience in every team member. Suppose one of your team members is facing some personal challenges. You acknowledge their problems and provide support. When they come across a setback again, they know that they will not be left alone. They have a leader who cares, understands, and helps everyone to get back on their feet.

CULTIVATING A CULTURE OF EMPATHY

It is not that tough to cultivate a culture of empathy in the workplace. Here are some of the ways in which you can showcase better empathy in the workplace and emerge as a successful leader.

Watching Out for Signs of Burnout in Others

Everyone who is a part of today's corporate world knows that work burnout is a genuine issue. In fact, it may pose a greater risk during times of excessive pressure and stress. Most people are stressed, trying to put in more hours of work than before. They find it hard to separate their home life and work life. Leaders who keep practicing empathy can easily identify the signs of overwork in their team members right before they enter the burnout phase. Burnout could lead to turnover or disengagement. Try to invest some more time every week to check in with your team and find out how they are trying to tackle the present workload. In case you find someone who is overworked, help them recover.

Demonstrating a Willingness to Provide Help to an Employee With Personal Issues

The line that exists between personal life and work life tends to be getting blurred in today's world. An empathetic leader can always understand that every member of their team is dynamic by nature who are dealing with personal issues while also taking care of their professional obligations. Leaders who practice empathy can recognize that it is their duty to support and lead all those in their team when they require it the most. One of the best ways to foster psychological safety in your team is to keep an open line of communication besides encouraging transparency. You will have to make your team members feel comfortable as they share something with you.

Showing Interest in the Hopes, Needs, and Dreams of Your Team Members

An important part of leading with empathy is about working to get to know the unique goals and needs of your team members. You will have to find out ways in which you can match assignments to contribute to employee satisfaction and performance. Employees who can see that their leader can recognize them like this will be more engaged in work. They will always be ready to go the extra mile. Keep in mind that demonstrating kindness in the workplace can always help boost culture and performance.

Showing Compassion When Someone Discloses a Personal Loss

True friendships and connections at the workplace matter. Empathetic leadership is a tool that you can always use to develop connections with all those team members you are privileged to lead. All of us experience personal loss in life. Even if you cannot relate to the loss experienced by one of your team members, you can at least make an effort to act empathetically and let them know that you are always there to support them.

HOW CAN ORGANIZATIONS ENCOURAGE EMPATHETIC LEADERSHIP?

It is true that some leaders are more empathetic naturally as compared to others. Such leaders can always have an upper hand over their peers who find it hard to express empathy. The majority of leaders belong to the middle and tend to be empathetic at times. Keep in mind that it is never a fixed trait. It is possible to learn empathetic leadership. If provided with enough support and time, leaders can easily improve and develop their skills of empathy with the help of training, coaching, or developmental initiatives. Organizations can always encourage an empathetic workplace and help leaders polish their skills of empathy in various ways.

- *Talking about empathy in the workplace to share its value*: Organizations will have to make leaders understand that empathy is important and it matters. There are leaders who tend to think of skills related to tasks like planning and monitoring to be more important in keeping the performance of their team members under check. However, it has been found that caring for, understanding, and developing other people is equally important, if not more, especially in the workplace culture of today's world. Organizations need to explain that providing attention and time to others can help in fostering empathy, which in turn can improve the performance of leaders and also their overall effectiveness.

- *Encouraging perspective-taking*: Leaders need to put themselves in the place of others consistently. For leaders, it involves considering the perspectives or personal experiences of the team members. The same thing can also be applied to solve issues, drive innovation, and manage conflicts.

- *Teaching listening skills*: In order to understand other people and sense all that they are feeling, leaders are required to be excellent listeners. They need to be active listeners who can let other people know they are being heard and also get to experience an understanding of issues and concerns. When a leader is a superb listener, the members of their team can feel respected. Trust in the team can be developed. To showcase empathy in the workplace, leaders need to concentrate on listening to get to know the actual meaning behind what other people are saying by focusing not only on the words but also on the values and feelings that are being showcased. It can be done with the help of nonverbal cues like facial expressions, pace of speech, tone, and gestures.

PREPARING FUTURE LEADERS: EMPATHY IN LEADERSHIP DEVELOPMENT PROGRAMS

Leadership development programs are required to include empathy training for preparing future leaders. But what is the reason behind it? Why should empathy training be included in leadership development programs? Here are some of the reasons:

- *Enhancing EQ:* Emotional intelligence (EQ) is important for a successful leadership. Empathy can be regarded as a cornerstone in EQ. It is about determining, understanding, and responding to emotions in others and oneself. Leaders who come with high EQ can manage their own emotions in a better way and develop true connections with team members. If empathy training is included in leadership development programs, participants can learn how to tune into their emotions and also the emotions of other people. They will get to find out the power of empathetic listening, which will improve their ability to relate to stakeholders and members of the team.

- *Fostering collaboration*: Leaders are required to excel in cross-functional partnerships and teamwork in today's collaborative work culture. An empathetic leader can easily develop an inclusive atmosphere where diverse perspectives are not only tolerated but are actively valued. A future leader who has undergone empathy training can easily understand the necessity of collaboration and inclusivity.

- *Developing trust*: Trust is important for effective leadership. Empathetic leaders have higher chances of developing and maintaining trust with the stakeholders and team. When the members of the team feel understood and supported, they will be more likely to have faith in their leader's vision and decisions. Participants in leadership development programs can learn to communicate in an authentic way, listen actively, and showcase true care for the well-being of other people. Such a trust-building skill is indispensable for the upcoming leaders.

- *Navigating diversity*: Workplace diversity is a fact of life. Future leaders are required to be equipped to get through the unique challenges and chances that come with global markets and diverse teams. Empathy can act as the bridge that can connect different experiences and perspectives.

So no matter if you are an aspiring leader or a leadership development program coordinator, keep in mind that empathy is the key to unlocking the leadership potential that you have inside yourself. It is a lot more than a skill. It is a glue that holds a diverse team together, a fuel that inspires motivation, and a compass that guides organizations in the direction of success.

CONCLUSION

I suppose leadership at one time meant muscles; but today it means getting along with people. −Mahatma Gandhi

You have reached the final page of the book, and I hope the journey through these pages was informative and fun to read. As we conclude this voyage, let us reflect on some of the lessons that we have learned from this book and the road ahead. The world of leadership has experienced a seismic shift. The days are gone when leadership was all about hierarchy and authority. In today's world, the most influential leaders are the ones who embrace empathy in all their approaches. We have learned that empathy is a lot more than a soft skill. It is a fundamental shift in how someone perceives leadership and the potential of the same. You can think of empathy as the currency of connection, the catalyst for change, and the bridge to understanding.

Empathy is not about being soft-spoken or emotional. All it involves is connecting, understanding, and caring for the team members in a true sense. Empathetic leaders tend to come with a rare capability to see the whole world through the eyes of other people. Keep in mind that empathy in leadership is not a one-size-fits-all kind of concept. It is versatile in nature. It can take various forms to match the requirements of different people and their situations. You can think of empathy as a multifaceted gem that can shine bright at times of crisis, nurtures collaboration, inspires innovation, and preaches inclusivity.

One of the best aspects of empathetic leadership is the ripple effect. When a leader leads their team with empathy, the actions they take can resonate far beyond their circle. Always remember that empathy breeds empathy, developing a culture where kindness and understanding are not the exception but a norm. Our journey through the pages of this book has been challenging as well. We have learned that practicing empathy can turn out to be demanding, specifically at times of conflict and adversity. As we end our journey, we must think about the future of empathetic leadership. I hope you have understood how this approach is no longer an option but a must-have in today's world. Future leaders are required to be empathetic to deal with the complexities of their time, to inspire greatness in others, and to develop trust.

Our journey has shown that empathetic leadership is not only a destination but a pursuit that would go lifelong. It would need constant growth, self-reflection, and adaptation. As we bid farewell to these pages, here's a task for you. No matter if you are an aspiring leader, a seasoned leader, or a person who just wants to make a positive impact, do not forget to practice empathy. Try to lead with empathy in your community, your workplace, and your home. Try to be the change that you desire to see in this world. Understand that empathy is a lot more than a concept to simply read about. It is more like a practice that you will have to do every day. Allow *Leading With Empathy* to be your guide, an inspiration source, and a reminder that in the world of leadership, empathy is like a thread that can weave connections, connect hearts, and develop a world where compassion and understanding are at the top of all.

Let me thank all of you for being with me on this short journey. May your life be filled with empathy, and I wish you grow into a leader who everyone else will follow. Never stop being empathetic, my fellow leaders!

REFERENCES

AIMS Education. (2015, March 18). *Tattoos in the workplace.* https://aimseducation. edu/blog/tattoos-in-the-workplace-healthcare-jobs-appearance-policies

Albert Einstein quote. (n.d.). A-Z Quotes. https://www.azquotes.com/quote/1345367

Bhan, S. (2023, January 5). *COVID taught us to be more empathetic: Microsoft CEO Satya Nadella.* CNBC. https://www.cnbctv18.com/technology/microsoft-ceo-satya-nadella-covid-19-pandemic-empathy-leadership-15578421.htm

Bourke, J., & Titus, A. (2019, March 29). *Why inclusive leaders are good for organizations, and how to become one.* Harvard Business Review. https://hbr.org/2019/03/why-inclusive-leaders-are-good-for-organizations-and-how-to-become-one

Bradberry, T. (n.d.). *Why you need emotional intelligence to succeed.* TalentSmartEQ. https://www.talentsmarteq.com/articles/why-you-need-emotional-intelligence-to-succeed/#:~:text=Of%20all%20the%20people%20we

Dwight D. Eisenhower quote. (n.d.). Pinterest. https://in.pinterest.com/pin/dwight-d-eisenhower-quote-leadership-is-the-art-of-getting-someone-else-to-do-something-you-want-done-because-he-want--979955200141073589/

Edú-Valsania, S., Laguía, A., & Moriano, J. A. (2022). Burnout: A review of theory and measurement. *International Journal of Environmental Research and Public Health, 19*(3), 1780. https://doi.org/10.3390/ijerph19031780

Ernst & Young. (2023, March 30). *New EY US Consulting study: employees overwhelmingly expect empathy in the workplace, but many say it feels disingenuous.* https://www.ey.com/en_us/news/2023/03/new-ey-us-consulting-study

Fallon, N. (2023, February 21). *35 Inspiring leadership quotes.* Business News Daily. https://www.businessnewsdaily.com/7481-leadership-quotes.html

Frank L. (2022, September 15). *46 remote work statistics employers need to know*. Stream. https://getstream.io/blog/46-remote-work-statistics/

Global Workplace Analytics. (n.d.). *How many people could work-from-home*. https://globalworkplaceanalytics.com/how-many-people-could-work-from-home

Greater Good in Education. (n.d.). *Empathy for students*. https://ggie.berkeley.edu/student-well-being/empathy-for-students/

Gupta, C., & Gupta, V. (2022, June 30). *How active listening can make you a better leader in the digital era*. ETHRWorld.com. https://hrsea.economictimes.indiatimes.com/news/industry/how-active-listening-can-make-you-a-better-leader-in-the-digital-era/92549846

Habash, C. (2022, February 1). *What is self-reflection, and why is it important for self-improvement?* Thriveworks. https://thriveworks.com/blog/importance-self-reflection-improvement/

Hunt, D. V., Layton, D., & Prince, S. (2015, January 1). *Why diversity matters*. McKinsey & Company. https://www.mckinsey.com/capabilities/people-and-organizational-performance/our-insights/why-diversity-matters

John C. Maxwell quote. (n.d.). BrainyQuote. https://www.brainyquote.com/quotes/john_c_maxwell_383606

Klug, K., Felfe, J., & Krick, A. (2022). Does self-care make you a better leader? A multisource study linking leader self-care to health-oriented leadership, employee self-care, and health. *International Journal of Environmental Research and Public Health, 19*(11), 6733. https://doi.org/10.3390/ijerph19116733

Lao Tzu quote. (n.d.). BrainyQuote. https://www.brainyquote.com/quotes/lao_tzu_121709

LaRusso, L. V. (2021, May 14). *Why is empathy an important communication skill in English*. LinkedIn. https://www.linkedin.com/pulse/why-empathy-important-communication-skill-english-how-vann-la-russo/

Leading Effectively Staff. (2023, January 28). *The importance of empathy in the workplace*. Center for Creative Leadership. https://www.ccl.org/articles/leading-effectively-articles/empathy-in-the-workplace-a-tool-for-effective-leadership/

Mahatma Gandhi quote. (n.d.). A-Z Quotes. https://www.azquotes.com/quote/105849

McQuaid, M. (2018, April 19). *Could compassion fuel your success?* Psychology Today. https://www.psychologytoday.com/us/blog/functioning-flourishing/201804/could-compassion-fuel-your-success

Miller, M. (2022, March 14). *The 3 parts of empathy: Thoughts, feelings and actions*. Six Seconds. https://www.6seconds.org/2022/03/14/3-parts-of-empathy/

Pollack Peacebuilding Systems. (n.d.). *Workplace conflict statistics 2023.* https://pollackpeacebuilding.com/workplace-conflict-statistics/

Quote by Dolly Parton. (n.d.). Goodreads. https://www.goodreads.com/quotes/39182-if-your-actions-create-a-legacy-that-inspires-others-to

Quote by Marcus Aurelius. (n.d.). Goodreads. https://www.goodreads.com/quotes/685844-whenever-you-are-about-to-find-fault-with-someone-ask

Quote by Sun Tzu. (n.d.). Goodreads. https://www.goodreads.com/quotes/233643-there-are-not-more-than-five-musical-notes-yet-the

Quote by William Howard Taft. (n.d.). Goodreads. https://www.goodreads.com/quotes/181116-i-ll-be-damned-if-i-am-not-getting-tired-of

Rosalynn Carter quote. (n.d.). BrainyQuote. https://www.brainyquote.com/quotes/rosalynn_carter_126340

Runyon, M. (2021, November 18). *How active listening can make you a better leader.* The Enterprisers Project. https://enterprisersproject.com/article/2021/11/how-active-listening-can-make-you-better-leader

The British Library. (n.d.). *Albert Mehrabian: Nonverbal communication thinker.* https://www.bl.uk/people/albert-mehrabian

The Economic Times. (2023, March 18). *JPMorgan's Jamie Dimon plays key role in bank rescue.* https://economictimes.indiatimes.com/news/international/business/jpmorgans-jamie-dimon-plays-key-role-in-bank-rescue-in-echo-of-2008/articleshow/98745106.cms?from=mdr

William Arthur Ward quote. (n.d.). BrainyQuote. https://www.brainyquote.com/quotes/william_arthur_ward_103463

Winston Churchill quote. (n.d.). A-Z Quotes. https://www.azquotes.com/quote/1428713

www.ingramcontent.com/pod-product-compliance
Lightning Source LLC
Chambersburg PA
CBHW061022220326
41597CB00017BB/2253